AF413777

Commentary on
Approximations to the Object

Bernstein, Pedro.
After Stone, Edmund.
Commentary on *Approximations to the Object* / Pedro Bernstein. — the ED.
— Eindhoven: Set Margins Press, 2025.
144 p. ; 19 x 14.5 cm. — (Commentary)

Printed on surplus stock originally intended for a discontinued series of titles withdrawn prior to publication.

Translated, annotated, and edited by Pedro Bernstein.

ISBN 978-90-835325-0-9

Designed Literature
CDD 809.93358

Original title of the text under commentary: *Approximations to the Object*, "A Tentative Towards a Literature of Things," first published in 1827 within the miscellany *Meditations on Literary Design*. Republished in part with the kind permission of B.P. Corder.

First edition, 2025
Design and cover by the author.

Commentary on
Approximations to the Object

Original text by Edmund Stone
Commentary by Pedro Bernstein

Published by Set Margins Press
Muntplein 14,
5611 TZ Eindhoven
The Netherlands

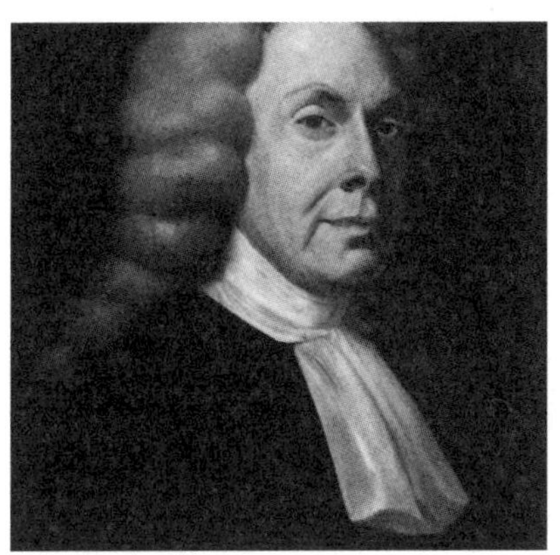

In loving memory of Edmund Stone
(1770 - 1812)

Table of Contents

Never before Printed in Folio
Published according to the Original Manuscripts

Approximations to the Object

A Tentative Towards a Literature of Things

EDMUND STONE

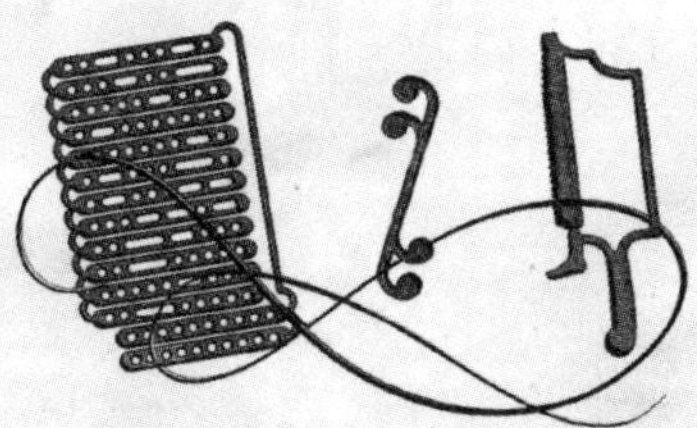

AN
EXCERPT FROM
Meditations on Literary Design

NORTHUMBERLAND:
PRINTED FOR B.P CORDER, PATERNMESTER ROW.
1827

Truth, whose mother is history, rival of time,
depository of deeds, witness of the past, exemplar and
adviser to the present, and the future's counselor.
—Pierre Menard, Author of the *Quixote*

Is that true wisdom which can comprehend that
there is a might-have-been which is more true
than truth, from which the dreamer, waking, says
not 'Did I but dream?' but rather says, indicts
high heavens very self with: 'Why did I wake
since waking I shall never sleep again?'
—William Faulkner, Absalom, Absalom!

Prologue to the First Edition

The design and literary research integrated in this volume was conducted from mid-2022 to mid-2023 as part of my dissertation at Parsons School of Design at The New School. I must admit that such literary design exercises led me to spend long hours at the Public Library of New York, where I eventually discovered Edmund Stone's incisive treatise *Approximations to the Object*, and thus to this very commentary, which arbitrarily reveals my reading, the enthusiasm of stumbling upon such source, and the sudden and selfish anguish of not having been its author.

It is important to mention that the fact that this research has been manifested in a text does not disqualify the instance of its objects and the incorporation of design within its literature, but rather ratifies it. Accordingly, I have produced a series of material replicas that both accompany and bifurcate from this writing, corresponding to the three case studies presented in the central body of the work. The incorporation of these objects is essential to inaugurating a possible literary design analysis, as they induce a material consciousness that interrogates the manner in which they reshape commentary while simultaneously extending Edmund Stone's central argument.

Consequently, I have concluded that a text functions both as a pretext and an expansion of the material world, and essentially as a vast ecosystem—as a space, a habitat, a refuge, a collection, a portfolio, a room, a boat, a chest, a suitcase, a bag, an attic, a closet, a box, an artifact, a host—capable of housing the sometimes impossible. While I hope this work is only a first approximation, or as Stone suggests, "A Tentative Towards a Literature of Things," I believe its function is allegorical to that of a bridge (or to the typographical symbols of the dash "–" or the ampersand "&") associating the discipline of the object with that of the text. Stone's piece, and analogously this commentary, manifest the thesis that given certain historical occurrences, literature (and its textual phenomena) has oriented itself towards objects and, therefore, that various artifacts have preceded the genesis of its meaning.

Although this study is not intended for the scientific field but rather the literary and hermeneutic one, it is important to acknowledge a tension (often noted by scholars) between Aristotle's conception of causality, as developed in *Physics*, and David Hume's critique of that very notion. While Aristotle grounded causality in rational principles that explain why one event necessarily follows another, Hume, in *A Treatise of Human Nature* (1739), argued that causality does not arise from reason but from the mind's habit of associating events, leading us to infer relations between objects or events. Stone, however, departed from both traditions. He showed less interest in how the mind perceived connections or transferred experience between events, and more in how material objects themselves preceded the mechanics of thought and meaning. In this sense, his study did not posit the design object as a cause in the Aristotelian or Humean sense, but rather as a pre-conceptual force; one that shaped literary articulation before interpretation.

Several decades after the publication of Hume's *Treatise*, Edmund Stone's upbringing took place in the northern English county of Northumberland, a region that remained relatively isolated from the rest of England due to its remote geography and underdeveloped infrastructure. Nearby, in the same northern territories, poet and writer Samuel Taylor Coleridge was born in 1772, just two years after Edmund Stone (1770–1812). The two would later reunite during their studies at Jesus College, University of Cambridge, where their early dialogues began to shape a shared metaphysical interest in how things come into being; showing a skepticism toward empirical causality and granting primacy to matter as the fundamental substance anterior to interpretation, imagination, and the operations of the mind.

Even if Samuel Taylor Coleridge did not write extensively about such a principle, his philosophical alignment with Stone was considerable; their early friendship maintained ideological affinities that undoubtedly induced a critical view towards emblematic figures of English academia. Like Stone, Coleridge maintained a significant divergence from the skeptical and empiricist philosophy that characterized many Enlightenment philosophers, including David Hume. In his work *Biographia Literaria*, Coleridge questioned the idea that all experience derives from observation and sensation (an explicit conviction in Hume), arguing in favor of an imaginative dimension in the process of knowing and understanding the world.

A similar argument emerges in the cases that Stone presents to his reader, exposed in this commentary, focusing on objects as pre-conceptual vessels that precede the meanings we assign to them—ideas that will be associated with the post-structuralist philosopher Jean Baudrillard to heighten the stratified and the phenomenological dimensions of things. In this way, both Coleridge and Stone defend the subjectivity of perception and knowledge, holding that the delight of reading the world cannot be reduced to mere sensory experience. In this sense, their approach differs from Hume's empiricist philosophy, which maintains that all ideas derive from experience and that causality is simply a habitual association formed through the repeated conjunction of events.

3

The latter point is entirely disregarded in Stone's treatise. Such objection explains that for Stone, in order to consider the repetition of an event, to trace an association of this type (a science of patterns), the events in question must have first been selected *a priori*, in the manner of a specimen, and must have been recognized as facts (to the detriment of others, the material with which one works is always the result of an arbitrary selection). His philosophy thus enacts a reversal of the linguistic turn: language does not generate reality; rather, objects generate the conditions for language to emerge. Subsequently, what emerges in his work is not a theory or a refutation of causal principles per se, but a reorientation towards isolated *object epistemai;* impious yet faultless material forces that have remained unarticulated within history's conception of the past, ineligible for their very repetition.

The reader might then assume that this work is a tribute to the writer, but it is, in fact, a homage to the experimental procedures that design exerted within his discourse.

Preamble: Intellectual Tidbits
on Edmund Stone

Given the intricate and convoluted nature of the literary design associations pertinent to *Approximations to the Object*, I will omit the author's interpersonal character as well as the romances of the scholastic figures mentioned in this commentary.

As a future reference for an avid reader interested in intellectual tidbits, Samuel Taylor Coleridge was one of the few poets who wrote personal accounts and biographies of contemporary figures of the time and maintained correspondence with Edmund Stone. Views like Stone's were considered radical and unconventional in his *milieu*, reasons that caused his unpopularity within the academic establishment. Such is also the case of Thomas Reid, the greatest advocate of common sense, whose work was neglected by the empiricist tendencies of the time and only recognized posthumously. One of the best-known works featuring Stone is *Biographia Literaria* (1817), an intellectual autobiography in which Coleridge explores his ideas about poetry, philosophy, and literature, published ten years after the writing of *Approximations to the Object* and five years after the ink poisoning that lead to Stone's death in 1812. This illness is said to have been caused by the period's habit of quill licking, wherein the very material activities central to 19th-century writing practice precipitated fatal toxicity.

Other works related to the radical intellectual circle of the time include *Anima Poetae: From the Unpublished Notebooks of Samuel Taylor Coleridge*, a collection of essays about poets and writers, and *Letters, Conversations, and Recollections for an Expanded Literature*, a collection of letters and conversations selected by Coleridge's friend and biographer, Thomas Allsop, regarding the literary design expansion that Stone's work produced.[1]

Author's Preface

Just as my discovery of Edmund Stone's treatise resulted in this commentary, I have come to consider literature, for the time being, as not only reading or writing, but more so the activities subsequent to these: those enduring conversations with colleagues or friends, the annotated margins, the notebooks saturated by inked thoughts, the scribbled quotes, the lost notes, an extensive browser history, multiple open tabs, Reddit threads, a dictionary, a thesaurus, a pen which tracks or annotates, the guilt of a young reader for inking a beautiful edition, the intrigue, the disagreements, the excitement produced by the discovery of a novelty, the desire for rereading, or the desire to read something very similar, the amazement or disappointment caused by an entirely fictional piece, the hidden references, the new possibilities, the sensation that reading is infinite and inexhaustible—in short, an endless source for imagining anew.

Therefore, my discovery, which has become in a way only visible in this commentary, should not be solely considered literature for its actively subsequent, enthusiastic, curious, and meditative character, but rather as a metaliterature of sorts that has become a personal peripety that no longer belongs to me, from which I free myself by sharing it, and in doing so, all I retain is the hope of instigating far more abundant, generous, obsessive, and enduring activities than my own.

I must specify that rereading certain texts by Jorge Luis Borges and Alexius Meinong has been, on a personal level, significant in shaping my interest in the disciplines of design and literature. As such, I have deliberately employed certain procedures throughout this writing: the inclusion of pre-existing quotes and images in Stone's work as a form of evidentiary support, the integration of philosophical references, the translation of Spanish sources that have yet to be officially translated into English, the reduction of an extensive *œuvre* to the confines of a commentary, and the emphasis on historical records that remain lost, left unfinished, or excluded, whether due to insufficient documentation, limited interest, or past subjectivities. (These same practices also abound in the works of many other authors referenced in this writing.)

Regarding the source, the writing of *Approximations to the Object* was completed in 1807 and, to this day, has yet to reach a significant readership. Throughout the 20th century the work was predominantly labeled in European regions as atheistic, satirical, and trivial, to the point of accusing Stone of not being its author, discrediting his studies, and condemning him for embarking on a purely speculative enterprise. Despite the fact that the original manuscript is said to have formed part of his miscellaneous reflections on *Designed Literature*, known as *Meditations on Literary Design*, these would not have been released until 1827 by B.P. Corder, a publishing house founded in Alnwick, Northumberland, in 1821, which intended to publish scholarly and esoteric works written primarily by authors from the region. This company continued operating until the end of the decade, when it was censored by English authorities who brought its founder, Barrett Packington, to trial, sentencing him as a radical atheist, blasphemer, and seditionist.

The hardships that the publishing system underwent at the end of the 19th century explain the clandestine routes elaborated to preserve the few circulating editions of suppressed texts in foreign institutions, such as the Public Library of New York, founded concomitantly. Despite its closure, B.P. Corder has been celebrated for having published a collection of undiscovered eccentric writers, such as Herbert Ashe and Silas Haslam, as well as for the sophisticated design of its limited catalogue.

As for the instances of magic enclosed in this volume, I have no right other than to allow the reader the same immersion in the narrative that I myself experienced, to trace the due parallels, the very ones I have inquired through Edmund Stone's meticulous work. Such sources, their onto-epistemological implications, the writing process, and the concepts coined for the surgical treatment that design exerts on literature will be unraveled in the epilogue of this thesis.

Note from the Publisher: On Provenance & Disputed Authorship

For reasons that remain unsettled, Edmund Stone's work has remained largely unexamined in contemporary literary studies. This edition presents a rigorous attempt to reconstruct his central thesis: that literary forms often derive from objects rather than the reverse.

Readers should note that certain aspects of Stone's argument remain subjects of ongoing debate. While some scholars regard his findings as eccentric yet insightful, others question the existence of verifiable records of his work prior to the 20th century. The publisher offers this edition in the spirit of intellectual curiosity and leaves all final judgments to the discretion of the reader.

Commentary on *Approximations to the Object*
(Northumberland, 1827) by Edmund Stone.

> In any given culture and at any given moment, the mutations
> between objects and language have proved to be interchangeable,
> yet too exposed to the vagaries of chance or imagery for it to be
> supposed that their history could be anything other than irregular.
> It was, in fact, the human attempt to make sense of that primary,
> incomprehensible, and once uninhabited space that led to the
> arbitrary archaeology of knowledge in Western thought.
>
> —Michel Foucault, *The Order of Things*, 1978

I owe this commentary to the conjunction of design and literature, to the stories that underlie objects, and to those objects that underlie stories.

On that account, this study foreshadows the affinity between form and format, things and their names, stories and spaces, authors' imaginations and their childhood toys, mathematics and the body, phonemes and graphemes. It is through the active engagement with said writing that I have been able to hypothesize that literature is a transversal line of time that does not exist without its space, a space of objects that are framed *by* and simultaneously frame the story *within*, a narrative that traverses[1] and intertwines the experience to become, codifying every object in the [frame] of the word; and its certainly ambivalent meaning.

The figure of the crossing and thus of a crossroads has long served as a site of contemplation that the Greeks used to express the idea of intersection and addition, purely spatial in its origin, which years later, towards the end of the 15th century, was transformed into the "+" symbol by the mathematician

---

[1] Note from the author: the Spanish word *travesía* phonetically resembles the English word traverse. The former means to journey, cross, or voyage. As such, journeys or itineraries are sometimes associated with forking paths and adventures.

Johann Widmann, in his book *Behende Und Hübsche Rechenung auff allen Kauffmanschafft* of 1489. The abstracted crossroads also gained popularity as a symbol for addition because of its resemblance to the Latin word "et," meaning "and." See the Greek map of its origin:

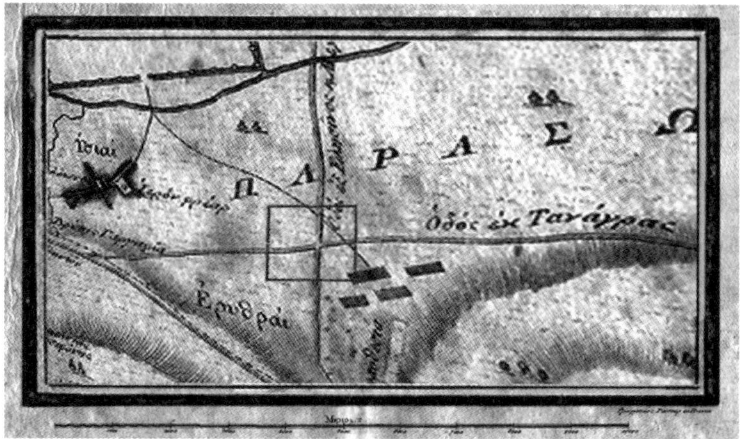

Fig. 1. *Orbis Pictus*, The World of Maps, Amonness Comenius, 1456.

Thereby, in search of an explanation for the similarity between space and meaning, between *what is* and *what becomes* narrated, between design and literature, I have disovered a literal (yet somewhat untended) edition of a text both poetic and anthropological, in the Crimson Hexagon Division at the Public Library of New York.[2]

The text, in some blasphemous way, vindicates the material being of objects as an obscure, defining precursor of the meaning they emanate (from the structures in which they are inserted), and illustrates, by means of several case studies, the intensities and flows between writing and things, or, on a lesser note, faces and their appearances.

----

[2] The Crimson Hexagon Division is a specialized research-focused section of the Public Library of New York, dedicated to curating and preserving books that are smaller than usual in format, richly illustrated, imbued with a sense of magic, and often regarded as possessing an almost all-powerful quality.

This treatise, titled *Approximations to the Object*[3] from 1827, whose subtitle states "A Tentative Towards a Literature of Things," written by the neglected English writer, critic, and thinker Edmund Stone, highlights how objects and their forms have preceded certain literary phenomena and consequently explain the formation of formats, fictions, and myths. Upon its reading, it becomes crucial to note that the relay system between narrative and experience evolves into a flow that transcends meaning, in such a way that the displacements through which knowledge is constituted (which are often considered real or truthful) are arbitrary, contextual, and ubiquitous. To be clear, both the utterance of a thing and the thing itself are generative of reality. In making, perceiving and enunciating, we assemble the world.

On discovering this volume, I understood the reason and attention the author places on things and their (morphological) forms.[4] From a postmodern or post humanist perspective, the contemporary world seems to have stratified knowledge to oblivion, obscuring any stable references. Stone, citing *Emile* by Rousseau, signals the dissolution of reference by stating:

"The sign has led to the neglect of the thing signified."[5]

Just as calluses on feet occur through friction and pressure caused by repetitive actions to the point of influencing how we walk, things and their fixed meanings (which oftenly become defining) have been abstracted to such a degree of opaqueness, blinding the way we think about them, and foremost, understand their possibilities whether real or imaginary.

---

[3] Other unrun editions have titled it haphazardly in latin: *Adpropinquationes ad Objectum* or *Tentamen ad Literaturam Rerum*, and in english: *A Mirror of Things: Towards a Tangible Literature*; *An Essay Toward the Writing of Things* and *On the Proximity of Things*.

[4] Note from the author: forms in Spanish, *formas*, alludes both to the shape and the manner of an object.

[5] In a premonitory note, Edmund Stone introduces *Discourse on the Origin and Basis of Inequality Among Men* (1755) written by the Genevan Philosopher Jean-Jacques Rousseau and explains: "We scarcely know how to give names to objects without enclosing them in some false idea or metaphysical abstraction. The language of metaphysics is but a language of signs, not of things; a language of appearances, not of realities. The material hiatus to which we are confronted, convoluted by humanity's insatiable linguistic gluttony; its compulsive habit of speaking with a mouth full, driven by the relentless desire to enunciate and define, serves only to suggest that any perspective on mind-independent objects can be as illusory and constructed as the objects themselves."

In his foreword, Stone declares that his civilization, and therefore the future civilization, has lost the sensitivity and "delight in the reading of things." He asserts that a writer never writes, and much less reads, but rather reveals and sculpts with words (a virtual technology of meaning) that which, in the absence of the letter, the mark, the order of succession that language imposes, remains uncannily present.[6] Even more remarkably, he recognizes that word and world are inextricably linked, offering an unprecedented understanding of the foundational relation between writer and designer—their distinctions and convergences in the fabrication of meaning and the shaping of reality.

Following this, the author explains that the craftsman, the modern-day designer, embodies ideologies into the object while the writer dissolves the strata on which it is founded to yield a specific treatment of reality. This correspondence points to a broader insight: artifacts might not simply be divine rafts of human concepts, but pre-discursive practices themselves—specific material arrangements that precede and provoke meaning.

It is as if, in seeking to undo the parasitic logic that privileges language over matter, Stone advances a view that underscores his notion of "material anarrativity." This concept highlights how events, as well as narrators in literature, often fail to capture the complexities and existential intricacies embedded in objects' beingness—say, highlight their spectral character, their immanent meaning, their capacity to pre-condition understanding. Ostensibly, the inconsistency of some literature with the inanimate has produced an incoherent, fragmented, and chaotic history, as it overlooked material realities outside the human and failed to register the structural forces of matter in the production of sense.

Thus, Stone's reparative endeavor has, over the last century, been reduced by some, to establishing a material lexicon for certain objects in literature.

---

[6] The German term *unheimlich*, included in Sigmund Freud's essay *The Uncanny* (1919), is the equivalent of the term "uncanny" in the author's native language. *Heim* means home; thus, *Unheimlich* means that which is not homely.

Though anchored in his own historical time, Stone's work resonates with literary currents from the turn of the last century, most notably the fantastic, which extensively explored the agency, complexity, and ontological richness of objects beyond the scope of human-centered narrative. Yet, even if his practice better fits the realm of theory, when the author sets out to access the artifacts of his study through their *thingness*, he remains unable to do so; for the obscure essence of objects resists comprehension and maintains their irreducibility to human understanding. Nonetheless, he effectively vindicates language as a medium that both manipulates and conditions the relationship between things and their meanings, cultivating in his readers a material consciousness that brings them closer to thinking *through* designed objects rather than merely *about* them.

Other writers have struck the same chord, implicitly addressing the impasse of things, as Borges writes in *Borges and I*: "Spinoza understood that all things want to persevere in their being; the stone eternally wants to be stone and the tiger a tiger," or as Clarice Lispector observes in *The Passion According to G.H.*: "That thing, whose name I don't know, was what I, looking at the cockroach, was already managing to call without a name."

In the introduction to his book, Stone critiques literature's depiction of material objects, arguing that it has often failed to recognize them as epistemic agents, thereby reinforcing an inherent deception in knowledge.

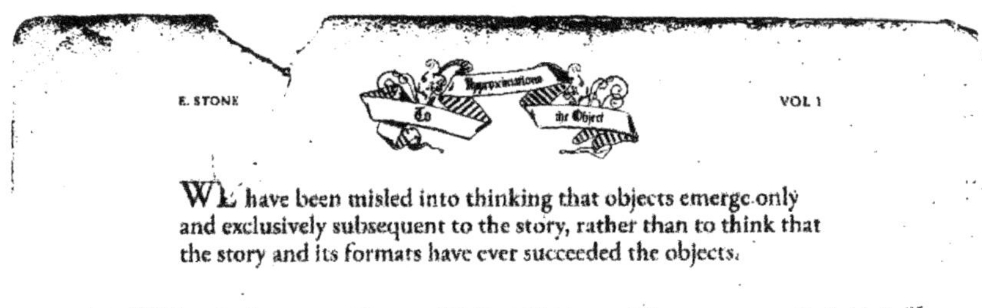

Fig. 2. Introduction to *Approximations to the Object*, 1827.

First and foremost rests the body, marked by a graphism, the innate matter that surrounds us, the materiality of things and their petty reasons for being appeased by the signaling of certain flows. It is as such that design intervenes as a code or signal. Consider, for instance, the rite of circumcision in the Judaic tradition, maps, uniforms or wedding rings, as examples of material interventions that indicate and circumscribe meaning. As Georges Perec exercises in *Penser/Classer* or Jorge Luis Borges in his essay titled *The Analytical Language of John Wilkins*, which is the pretext that led Michel Foucault to write *The Order of Things*, humans construct arbitrary taxonomies of meaning under a disturbing illusion of order, or labyrinths whose walls, built by themselves, trap them.[7]

Such is the paradox of design: while it organizes and signals, it constructs and simultaneously conceals. In this sense, design can be regarded as an architecture of meaning, an armamentarium of heuristics; devices of manipulation by which humans transpose certain material inferences onto reality. Yet these inferences are rarely neutral, they embed intentions, generate consequences, and establish the conditions for the world to be imagined, built and navigated.

A study of designed literary forms, especially those concerning concrete object phenomena preceding the emergence of text, had not been fully articulated between the domains of design and literature until Stone recognized

---

[7] While writing this commentary, I revisited lectures in which Gilles Deleuze discusses societal codes, much as design aesthetics or language shape identity and behaviors, illustrating this through the example of how different hairstyles are codified to reflect various social roles: "What happens on the body of a society? Flows, always flows. A person is always a cut of flow, a starting point for the production of flows and a destination point for the reception of flows. Or rather, an intersection of many flows. Flows of all kinds. A person's hair, for example, can go through many stages: the hairstyle of a young woman is not the same as that of a married woman, nor is it the same as that of a widow. There is a whole code of the hairstyle. The person, in as much as she carries her hair, presents herself typically as an interceptor in relation to the hair flows that exceed her, that go beyond her case. These hair flows are codified in different ways: widow's code, young woman's code, married woman's code, etc. Ultimately, this is the essential problem of codification and territorialization: always codifying the flows. And as a fundamental means, marking people, for they exist at the intersection, at the cutting points of the flows. Therefore, marking people is the apparent means for the deepest of functions." (Author's translation.) Gilles Deleuze, *Derrames entre el capitalismo y la esquizofrenia,* 2nd ed., trans. Pablo Ariel Ires & Sebastián Puente (Cactus, 2021), 23.

such material anarrativity and wove a historiography that interrogated how the fields of objects and texts converge through meaning-making techniques.

However to reduce Stone's treatise to merely establishing a material lexicon for objects would be faulty. His work not only defends the thesis that certain design objects have preceded literature (or certain semantic systems), but also anticipates sensibilities later pursued by other thinkers, especially one of object-oriented philosophy's major advocates, Graham Harman. Had Stone not introduced a more nuanced engagement with objects during the 19th century, Object-Oriented Ontology (OOO) might not have emerged as it did.

In this sense, Stone's critique of Hume's empiricist reductionism, which treats objects as mere sensory appearances, marked an important step forward. Rather than reducing objects to bundles of impressions, Stone insists that objects precede and condition language rather than being solely constructed by it. In doing so, he intends to rescue objects from ontological simplification, restoring their role as active epistemic agents in the formation of meaning.

That said, contemporary object-oriented theories diverge from Stone's realist materialism, which Graham Harman classifies as part of philosophy's tendency towards "overmining"—the idea that objects exist only in their appearances, relations, qualities, or effects. In response to such reductive tendencies, Harman advances what he provocatively terms "realism without materialism," emphasizing the autonomy of objects beyond both their underlying substance and external manifestations.

What should still be noted is that while Stone undoubtedly critiques the material anarrativity of certain literary discourses, his study exposes particular unresolved nuances, as his focus is not on the distinction between object and writing, or object and subject, but rather on how meaning emerges through a constant interplay between materiality and language. For Harman, instead, all objects are not simply lacking a proper language; they exceed all linguistic and conceptual grasp. Thus, while Stone cultivated a material consciousness that brings readers closer to thinking *through* and *with* objects, Harman pushes

19

further, insisting that objects remain irreducible to human sense-making; not just misunderstood, but ultimately unknowable in their full reality.

Regardless of such disparities, Stone's inquiry did not specifically concern accessing an object's reality but rather aimed to create an anthology exploring the flows between design and literature. While his endeavour still projected human qualities onto non-human entities (as the objects in his study are seen to precede textual phenomena) his approach was progressive for its time, marking a turn from the anthropocentric to the anthropomorphic, shifting the focus from humans to artifacts (as apprehended by humans).

A lingering question that commonly arises in the reading is whether Stone's notion of material anarrativity could have referred to the linguistic gulf of objects, which I believe is paradoxically shown to shrink through the active textual engagement he offers. If such is the case, Stone could be regarded as a pioneer in recognizing that the fabrication of objects, as seen in the field of design and incorporated into literature, can act as powerful agents to push language and reality beyond its existing limits; tools for isolating and bringing into focus key conceptual issues, demanding and coining new ter-minology, presupposing novel relationships for epistemic treatments, and fostering material networks that contaminate and diverge the way discourse is constructed. In his work, material objects are seen to have intrinsically manifested literary phenomena, even prior to being abducted into linguistic symbols, structures, and systems. Such a possibility gestures towards a lan-guage embedded *in* and withheld *by* objects; one that, though never fully accessible to humans, still affects, suggests, and conditions human experience through its phenomena.

In the following pages, I will elucidate such arguments by including passages from the author explaining the origin of the Shakespearean sonnet, accom-panied by images adjacent to such descriptions, and later proceed to examine additional case studies.

The Shakespearean Sonnet
& The Object-Sonnet

Shakespeare's sonnets are a set of 154 poems in the English sonnet's strophic form, employing iambic pentameter to address themes such as love, beauty, politics, and mortality. These themes are anecdotal, but as a great admirer of the author, I long to encounter variations of the object to be described in this essay, capable of hinting at their themes through varied materialities; as if different materials could evoke a range of emotions, forms, or rhythms. By this, I mean that an object made of stone would lend itself far more, for its weight and texture, to a semantic field associated with mortality rather than with love. In fact, in the Talmudic tradition, stones, not roses, are left on tombstones when visiting the dead.

Setting aside these preferences, Shakespeare's sonnets were likely composed over several years before being published in full in 1609, with the exception of the first two drafts, which saw multiple iterations and remained unresolved until years later. These initial versions had already circulated a decade earlier in select editions of a more informal miscellany from 1599 titled *The Passionate Pilgrim*, a publication that would later be partially discontinued due to numerous misattributions introduced during its printing. The confusion surrounding these volumes has been attributed primarily to its printer, William Jaggard, who is believed to have accidentally combined texts from various manuscripts held in his printing house. (Whether this conflation was an error of attribution, a commercially motivated interpolation, or part of a broader project of textual rearrangement remains unclear.)

According to certain 18th-century Stratfordian Scholars, the logical scandal intensified when members at the Lord Chamberlain's Men (the acting company to which Shakespeare belonged) discovered circulating folios bearing the title *The Passionate Pilgrim by W. Shakespeare* which mistakenly bound together a sequence of Shakespearean sonnet spreads with an incomplete and unreleased quarto tract from a work that Sir Francis Bacon had in press at the time. Despite there being a call to suppress these apparently "faulty" poetry collections, efforts to remove them from circulation were not entirely successful. Centuries later, Edmund Stone's treatise revealed the continued existence of one such misprinted edition. The misprinting case of *The Passionate Pilgrim* has since then been regarded as the first case to question Shakespeare's literary legitimacy, suggesting that the sonnets, and even some plays, lack a clear line of provenance.

Indeed, it would be dubious to claim that the sonnets' history was ever transparent, as the conditions of their publication remain uncertain to this day.

In this context, Stone's sturdy insights are particularly intriguing as they brought new light to the matter by elucidating the textual anomalies through design. Among his most compelling findings was the surviving misprinted folio of *The Passionate Pilgrim* from 1599, including the Shakespearean sonnet spreads and Bacon's unfinished tract. Through this volume, Stone was able to salvage the earliest variations of Sonnet I, "To the Sonnet Wrought of Walnut's Hart," and Sonnet II, "When First Fair Will Beheld the Form," both of which were omitted from the later edition titled *Shakespeare's Sonnets,* published by Thomas Thorpe in 1609, and have since remained discontinued throughout the author's repertoire. However, Stone draws the reader's attention to subtle traces of their existence, which continue to echo in a cryptic dedication of the 1609 volume—inscribed then by a certain T. T. (presumably the editor, Thomas Thorpe)—that invokes a mysterious object-sonnet as "the only begetter" of the poems. The origin of this object went largely unnoticed throughout literary history until Edmund Stone's prolific research in *Approximations to the Object* brought it to light.

Detailed in his prose, he accounts for how certain archives belonging to Shakespeare's family heritage led him to find an object of kinship to the inscription. This object, alluded to in the early sonnets from *The Passionate Pilgrim* and honored in Thorpe's 1609 dedication, becomes evident through a note dated to Shakespeare's childhood, marked by his father,

John Shakespeare, an artisan and glover of the time. The document, somewhat transfigured and blurry, appeared to have been written with an iron-based ink, explaining its provenance: a hand-carved gift from father to son.

Such an artifact, Stone hints, was not only a domestic keepsake but also the physical referent to the written sonnets, an object crafted from a type of wood that would have been discontinued in England centuries later. (From the Middle Ages through the Industrial Revolution, England predominantly utilized native woods such as oak and walnut for domestic purposes, which would eventually be replaced by imported Baltic pine as international trade expanded.)

Replicas of the object have since been identified in circulating Shakespearean design archives, where efforts have been made to recreate the symbolic representations of the object-sonnet. This motif, imprinted in select folios of Shakespeare's rarest first editions, featuring engravings of the poet holding the artifact, has circulated within cultural institutions as a literary fetish. Following is a photograph showing an edition of *The Passionate Pilgrim* from 1599, displayed alongside a walnut replica of the object-sonnet, exhibited at the Public Library of New York from February 1, 1990, to Febraury 30, 1993. Also included herein are the title page of Thomas Thorpe's *Shakespeare's Sonnets*, as included in *Approximations to the Object*, and the full extent of his dedication.

[See next spread]

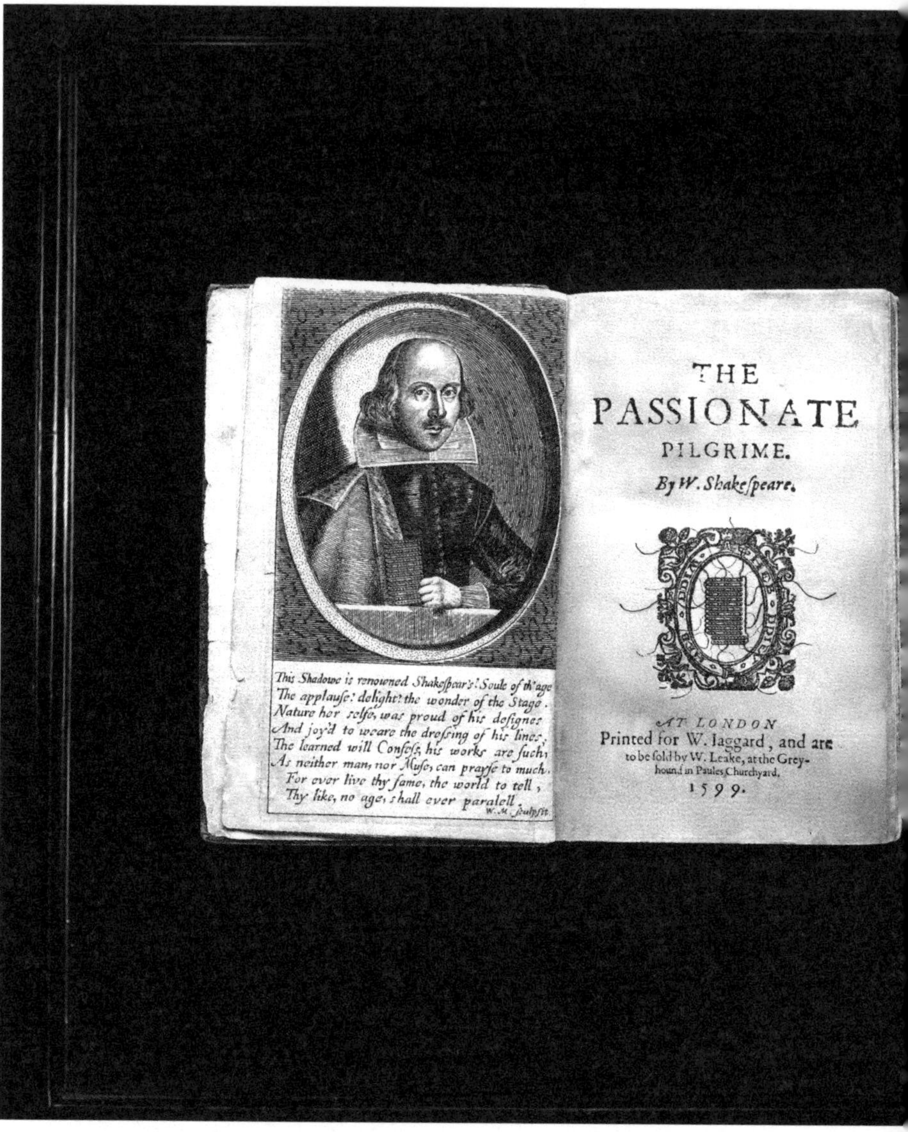

Fig. 1. A misprinted edition of *The Passionate Pilgrim* issued
in 1599 exhibited next to a replica of an object-sonnet at the
Public Library of New York.

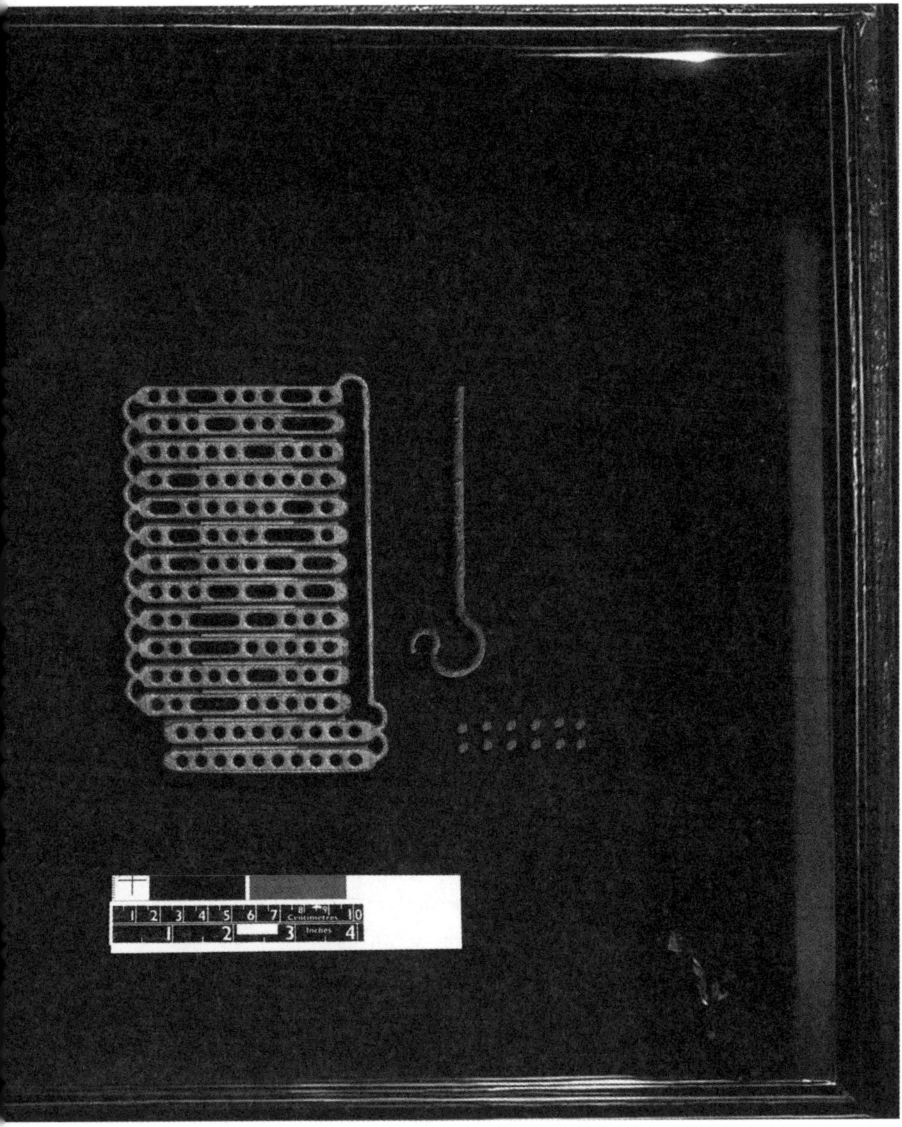

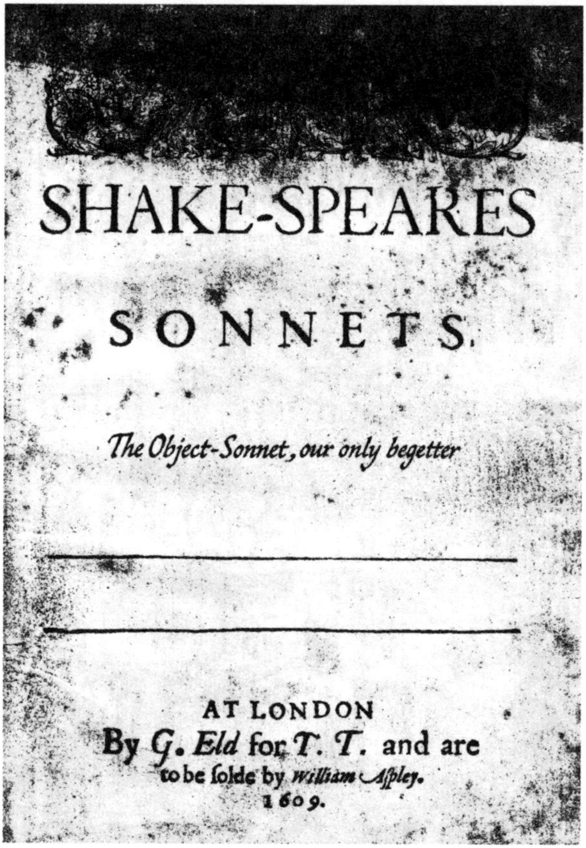

Fig. 2. Title page of *Shakespeare's Sonnets* as featured in *Approximations to the Object*, reproduced from a rare copy held in the Trinity Collection near Cambridge.

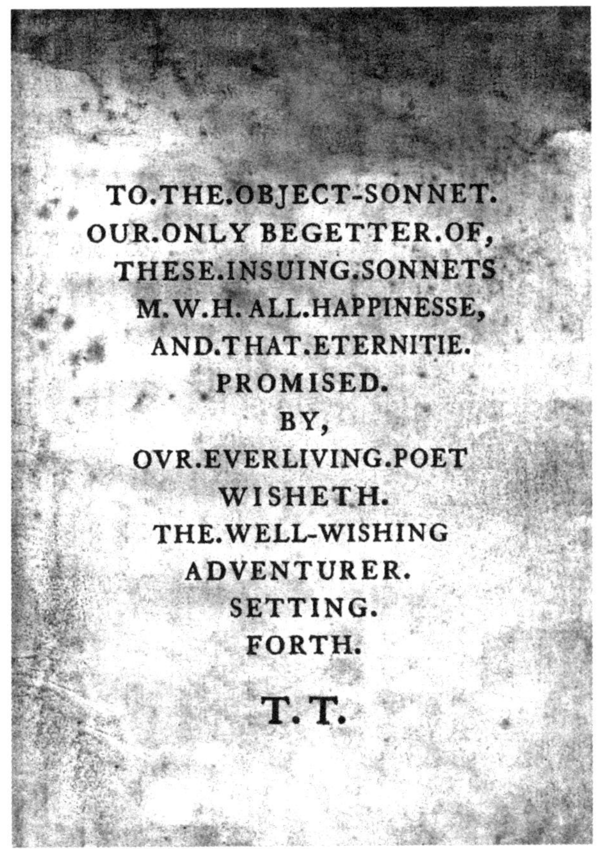

Fig. 3. Folio from Thomas Thorpe's 1609 edition of *Shakespeare's Sonnets*, containing the full dedication.

In his treatise, Stone maintains that the form of said object explains, in turn, the format that Shakespeare would later engrain in his poems:

> The object is composed of fourteen wooden verses, figured in forms that resemble those of a rectangle with curved corners; each verse chained in turn to the next by concave ligaments that culminate in a final pair, of two indented verses that restore themselves at the beginning of the poem. In each verse, there are circular holes, presented individually or jointly, seemingly alluding to the syllabic structure of each line, articulated in the simple or compound words of a Shakespearean sonnet. (Stone, 1827, p. 33, §§10–11)

Finally, Stone observes that the misalignment of the last two verses, the concluding *volta* of the object-poem, is mirrored indentically in the structure of the Shakespearean sonnet, as its last two lines also appear textually indented at the end to signify the subversion of the pre-established order in the poem, imbuing in it a sense of surprise, rigor, and elegance. Thus, whether intentional or not, the object's layout precedes the composition of the text, implying a material poetics (one that prescribes the basis for its semantic structure).

The author does not fully conclude whether there would be a way to interact with this object, aside from the way a child plays with a toy, or if such an object postulated any particular reading or tracking of reading through touch, trace, perforation or tactile punctuation. As a side note, similar systems would have been advanced in warlike developments centuries later. Such is the case of Charles Barbier de la Serre, who served in the French army from 1784 to 1792 and is best known for developing the technology that preceded Braille, known as *écriture nocturne*. Given that many soldiers were killed in the middle of the night when the light they used to read maps or orders exposed them to enemies, Barbier's work consisted of developing a raised-dot writing system as a solution requested by Napoleon Bonaparte to devise forms of silent communication. Years before such realization, Barbier would have attended a conference about the Greek historian Polybius and his system known as the Polybius Square, which proposed transmitting messages over great distances with the help of torches. Although the army did not widely adopt Barbier's system, Louis Braille adapted it to create a novel reading system for people with visual impairment in the mid-19th century. Barbier's contributions formed part of a broader military interest in silent and remote communication, also pursued by contemporaries such as Claude Chappe, the French engineer who invented an optical semaphore system that transmitted messages over great distances, illustrated below.[1]

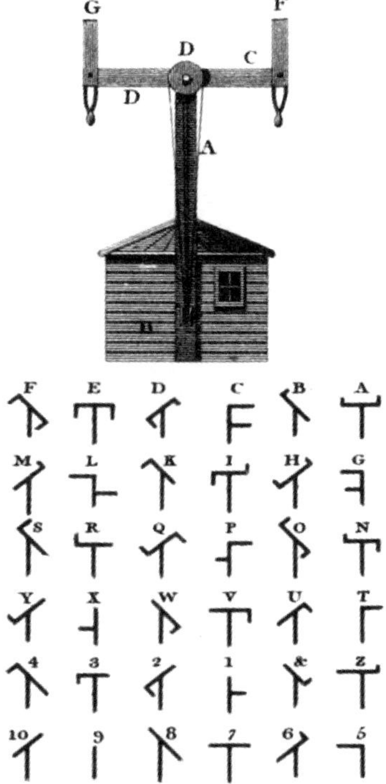

Fig. 4. Semaphore alphabet equivalents diagram, illustrating Chappe's attempt to systematize long-distance silent communication through graphic signs.

---

[1] Other writing and reading systems like the Inuit maps, the Quipu, or Braille are of significant comparison with the object-sonnet instrumentalized in William Shakespeare's childhood. These systems exercise the possibilities of graphic signs intended for the finger, instead than for the eye, and have expanded the ways of cognizing meaning.

Following this parallelism, I shall also include the scan of the original image inquired into by Edmund Stone in *Approximations to the Object* (attested by a provincial notary operating in the outskirts of Oxford):

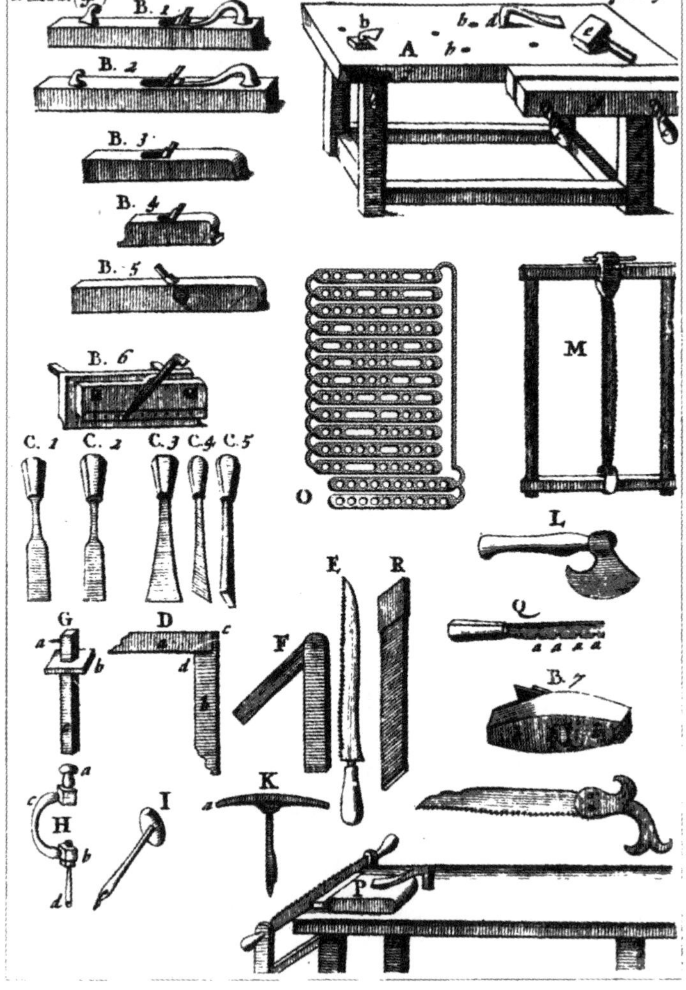

Fig. 5. John Shakespeare's toolsheet,
Approximations to the Object, 1827.

Detailed in this inventory, developed to train young artisans, are the wood-working hand tools belonging to John Shakespeare's craft. Stone pays special attention to the object cataloged as "O," understood as the object-sonnet, predating William Shakespeare's sonnet writing. He further reminds the reader that the limited history of this object "remains yet to be further studied" and laments the survival of only a few precisely dated specimens. Anonymity and displacement, he notes, are constitutive characteristics of the history of 17th-century tools. Indeed, a tool's usefulness is apt to continue through many years and the hands of several generations of artisans, leading to the frequent erosion of its origin. It follows, then, that a tool's function reassesses itself when introduced to new disciplines. In this specific case, the provenance of such an artifact, tool, or presumably toy, does not mainly concern the standardization of such in the discipline of woodworking but also in literature. Therefore, I find it relevant to propose an exhaustive literary design analysis of Shakespeare's sonnets through his toy. Some immediate questions that arise are: When did the forms of English woodworking tools begin to shape the literature of that same continent? What set of methods does said artifact entail, and what cognitive or reasoning processes come into play? In a similar manner, what other tool forms could have predominated William Shakespeare's childhood imagination, and, if ever, did any other tools achieve such distinctive influence on the practices of other writers? In attempting to resolve these questions, one faces ever-diminishing liter-ature along with a scarce poetic analysis (or understanding) of such tools.[2]

31

---

[2] In mathematics, the object-sonnet has been compared to the abacus for its form and mnemonic function. Although these objects do not appear in the writings of Gottfried Wilhelm Leibniz, Stone establishes an aesthetic and arithmetic relationship between Shakespeare's poetic interaction with the object and a mathematician's interaction with a calculator. Stone references Leibniz's *De Arte Combinatoria* and its concept of external autonomous thought, while also tracing a conceptual prec-edent in Ramon Llull's *Ars Magna* (a combinatorial logic system developed to uncover theological truths through symbolic rotation). Just as all concepts are combinations of a finite number of words, words are combinations of letters, and the sonnet an assemblage of syllables, the object-sonnet and other calculating machines, such as the abacus or Leibniz's *Stepped Reckoner*, prompted cognitive processes through material form, enabling both mnemonic and compositional autonomy. Stone posits that the senses instigated by such objects, both poetic and numerical, utmost musical, may have led to new abstract truths. Therefore, much like the abacus might have structured numerical thought through tactile patterns, the object-sonnet, according to the author, could have granted autonomy to poetic structures, functioning as both a tool for composition and memory.

After the inclusion of the previous sheet, Edmund Stone concludes the first chapter of his treatise by outlining the complete set of sonnets. He emphasizes the significance of the two early drafts appearing exclusively in select editions of *The Passionate Pilgrim*, paying homage to the object-sonnet that inspired their textual form; versions that were later omitted from subsequent editions such as the final *Shakespeare's Sonnets*.

Despite their absence, the final publication of *Shakespeare's Sonnets* from 1609 presents:
• The first 17 sonnets, addressing a young man and urging him to marry and have children so that his beauty can be transmitted to the next generation. (This group of poems is known as the *Procreation Sonnets*.)
• Sonnets 18 to 126, addressing a young man as well, but now expressing the love that the lyrical voice feels for him.
• Sonnets between 127 and 154, written for the lyrical voice's lover, expressing his love for her and dealing with themes such as infidelity, the resolution to control lust, and so forth.

(Versions of Sonnets I and II from The Passionate Pilgrim remain excluded from Thorpe's edition and hence from this list. In spite of these two poems being the first to pay tribute to their origin, the object-sonnet does remain thematically and tacitly present through Thorpe's 1609 dedication.)

Also included as a reference are the first two versions of the allegorical sonnets, elemental to Stone's study, apropos of the relationship between form and format in Shakespeare's practice.

Sonnet {I}

O slender frame, thou chamber of the muse,
Thy measured breath gives form to thought and fire,
In thee, the restless spirit finds its cues,
And ink, once dumb, ascends like sacred lyre.
Fourteen thy steps, each foot in counted grace,
Where reason dances close with passion's flare,
Thy turns conceal as much as they embrace,
And mask confession in the tightest snare.
Thou art no carven wood nor idle shell,
But living law where soul and sound convene,
A lattice wrought where silent wonders dwell,
The verse's vessel and its voiceless queen.
    Thou dost endure, though all the world forget
    A shape the tongue remembers, even yet.

Sonnet {II}

Thou art of wood, yet hold'st a breath more deep
Than forest winds or fife of rustling leaves;
Thy grain, a script where unborn words do sleep,
And every curve the tongue in silence grieves.
No sap remains, yet still thy fibers sing,
In thee, the blood of speech doth rise and fall;
Each joint a beat, each hollow pulse a ring,
As though some Muse were prison'd in thy wall.
No hand did ink thee, yet thy frame is lore,
A metered code in matter's secret tongue;
Ere man could rhyme, or number beauty's score,
Thy form in shadow'd groves was softly sung.
    Thou speak'st in wood, where letters none are seen,
    And mak'st of breath a law, unseen, unseen.

As a possible poetic arithmetic deviation, I have harnessed certain conceptual resources from poetry and fundamental mathematical operations featured in *Bead Arithmetic* by KWA Tak Ming to extend a literary and design-based analysis of this phenomenon. If one were to examine John Shakespeare's tool-sheet and analyze particularly his abstract pedagogical instrument, it might be supposed that such an object would have preceded one of the 154 sonnets included in Shakespeare's final poetry collection.

According to Stone's universal conventions, a Shakespearean sonnet follows the object-sonnet structure, consisting of 14 verses, each written in iambic pentameter and adhering to the ABABCDCDEFEFGG rhyme scheme. Despite his intriguing findings and studies in arithmetic, Stone's lack of graphological analysis left unfinished the deciphering of what the real writing might have conveyed. Consequently, there remains no definitive account identifying which particular poem is supposed to correspond to this material predecessor; Stone only details, as previously discussed, that the early versions of Sonnets I and II explicitly allude (in a textual rather than material manner) to their origin. While I cannot guarantee that this artifact fully adheres to the conventional function of writing, it's nonetheless tempting to exercise a functional reading. Hence, I have proceeded to count the words and syllables across all Shakespearean sonnets ultimately to conclude that the object-sonnet Stone studies serves precisely as the material precursor of Sonnet XVIII.

The wonder and possibility of there being other existing (or documented) object-sonnets—each with distinct material or structural qualities, capable of preceding non-existent poetic structures and verses—lingers within Stone's short, vital, and partial practice, and remains a source of intrigue for me as a reader and design researcher. The delineated analysis I have outlined to assert the object's kinship to Shakespeare's Sonnet XVIII is illustrated hereafter.

[See next spread]

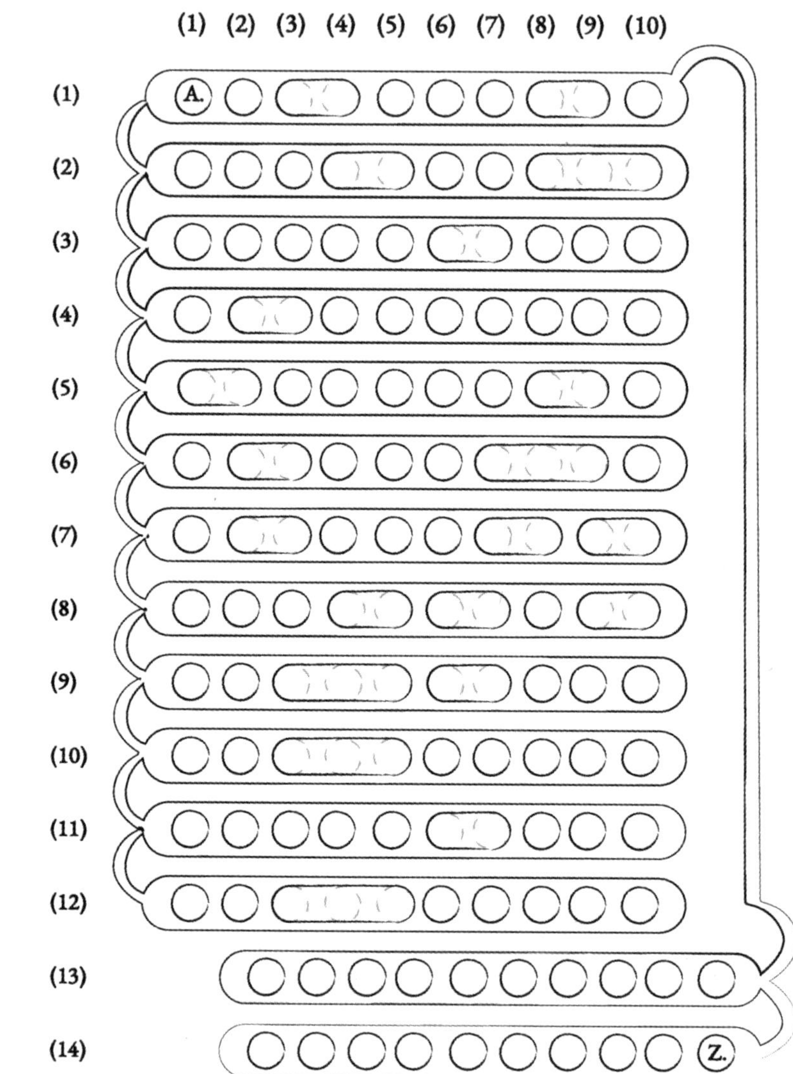

*If A is Hole №1, Z is Hole №114

Line №	Line Text	Words	Syllables
(1)	Shall I com pare thee to a sum mer's day?	(8)	(10)
(2)	Thou art more love ly and more tem per ate:	(7)	(10)
(3)	Rough winds do shake the dar ling buds of May,	(9)	(10)
(4)	And sum mer's lease hath all too short a date;	(9)	(10)
(5)	Some time too hot the eye of hea ven shines,	(8)	(10)
(6)	And oft en is his gold com ple xion dimm'd?	(7)	(10)
(7)	And ev ery fair from fair some time de clines,	(7)	(10)
(8)	By chance or na ture's chang ing course un trimm'd;	(7)	(10)
(9)	But thy e ter nal sum mer shall not fade,	(7)	(10)
(10)	Nor lose pos ses sion of that fair thou ow'st;	(8)	(10)
(11)	Nor shall Death brag thou wan ders't in his shade,	(9)	(10)
(12)	When in e ter nal lines to time thou grow'st;	(8)	(10)
(13)	So long as men can breathe or eyes can see	(10)	(10)
(14)	So long lives this, and this gives life to thee.	(10)	(10)
		(114)	(140)

If such parallelism follows, the object-sonnet effectively illustrates:

• Fourteen curved rectangular verses prefiguring the 14 lines of a written sonnet, with the last two showing an indentation, both realized in its respective material and linguistic structures.

Taking this a step further, by mapping the hole-to-word parallelism, I have deduced that there must be 114 words (matching the 114 holes). If these are to accurately follow the syllabic structure of the object, the words would diversify into different variants—simple or compound, as Stone noted—accounting for a total of 140 syllables.

Hence the prior metrical analysis, juxtaposed with a visual analysis of the object-sonnet's form, proves that:

• Holes appear along each verse, stipulating the number of words per line, with spatial variations shaped by the number of syllables and the complexity of the words to which they belong. These holes effectively prefigure the disposition of the monosyllabic, disyllabic, and trisyllabic words in Sonnet XVIII.
• The last two indented lines of the object-sonnet mark the rhyming couplet, visually reinforcing the sonnet's formal closure.

Thus, it can be concluded that both the object-sonnet and Sonnet XVIII contain:

• 114 visible holes that prefigure 114 words
• 140 syllables, distributed across 114 varied holes carved in the object-sonnet, mirrored one-to-one in the 140 syllables that make up the 114 simple and compound words of the written sonnet.[3]

---

[3] As a formal and material nightmare, the object-sonnet—even while requiring a somewhat quantifiable total of 140 syllables distributed across 14 lines—gives rise to an infinite exponential combination of words, drawn from any of the universe's varied languages, that, if ordered in a particular sequence, are capable of fitting within the object's structure. This implies that an infinite number of Shakespearean sonnets, preceded by said artifact, remain to be articulated. As such, the object's abstract formalism has been of interest to Stone for its infinite and disparate generative nature.

Therefore, following these poetic arithmetic procedures (which highlight poetry as a mathematics of the tongue and of the word, with a page as its body) it can be argued that such an object, when analyzed as both an abstract mathematical instrument and a physical tool, is the material forerunner of Shakespeare's Sonnet XVIII,[4] aligned in both structure and content.[5]

Prior to concluding the first section of this commentary, which specifically concerns the affinity between form and format, I must emphasize that the first sonnet came into being in Italy during the Middle Ages. One of the most recognized writers involved in the first development stage of the sonnet was Dante Alighieri, author of *The Divine Comedy,* of which Stone makes no mention in his book. Neither does Stone refer to Francesco Petrarca, a scholar, and poet of early Renaissance Italy, who imprinted a definite form to the sonnet that became popular and transcended its society to become, precisely, the "Petrarchan sonnet." Unlike the Shakespearean sonnet, where the author focuses his analysis, the Petrarchan sonnet consists of 14 hendeca-syllable verses (composed of eleven syllables) divided into two stanzas of four verses (a quartet) and two stanzas of three verses (a triplet).

---

[4] The textual history of Shakespeare's sonnets makes it difficult to verify whether the full collection was ever published or if the sonnets were ever read in the correct order. The sonnets as we know them today follow a specific sequence, but it remains unclear whether that order reflects Shakespeare's intentions or if it was arranged by his editor, Thomas Thorpe. In this way, the placement of the most celebrated sonnet (XVIII) still appears completely arbitrary to this day.

[5] Even while subjecting the object-sonnet to a literary design analysis, or as Stone suggested "an approximation to the object," we must remain clear-minded that we are playing this game through its phenomena, by making it an object of the senses: representations of *unknown somethings.* In doing so, we are unable to address its *noumenon*—the object as it exists independently of human perception. Thus, the attributes drawn from the object-sonnet overextend certain reflections of its appearance, of its surface phenomena at the macroscopic level, onto literature, thereby shaping unprecedented poetic-material resources within a field whose rules are generally linguistic. Such an extension, poses an incongruity in affirming a "material anarrativity," precisely because it negates the object's material muteness by endowing it with sense, with poetry, with meaning. Stone's uncovering of the object-sonnet thus creates a designed friction between objects and language, for even as we reveal their manifestations, their status as things-in-themselves remains fundamentally unknowable, obscured by the illusion of meaning that we impose upon them (constrained by the limitations of our sensory and conceptual apparatus). Nevertheless, even if the object-sonnet was not studied as a *noumenon*—neither by Stone nor by myself—this omission serves only to highlight its significant impact on the poetic field, opening pathways for new abstractions and enabling a poetic ambivalence capable of diverting the paths taken towards *unknown somethings.*

I offer then, as part of this research-based *Designed Literature*, a sketch made to depict what could have been a Petrarchan object-sonnet, following the previous literary outline, as an attempt to fill in the gaps of Edmund Stone's investigation.[6]

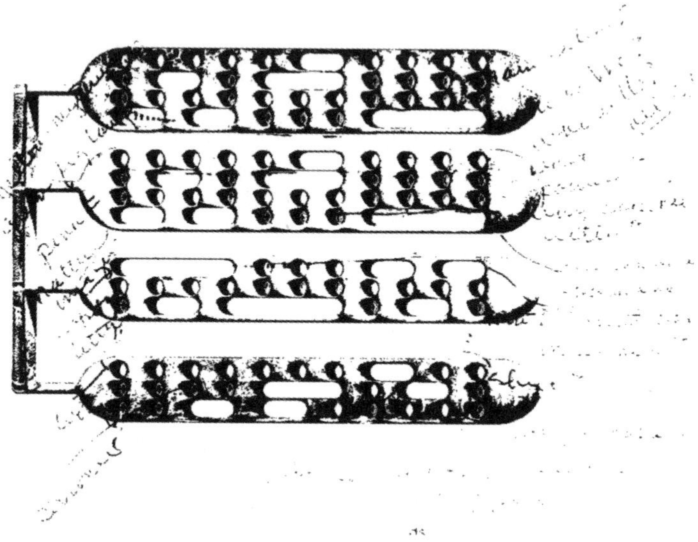

Fig. 6. Sketch of a Petrarchan object-sonnet.

[6] Such omissions have raised questions about the intentionality of Stone's treatise, especially since the true origin of the sonnet can be traced to Giacomo da Lentini, a Sicilian poet from the 13th century. Da Lentini, a notary for King Frederick II of Sicily, is regarded as the first to craft the sonnet. While Petrarch and Shakespeare have been celebrated for their mastery of the form and its popularity, it is important to recognize that the invention of the sonnet predates them and may have even drawn from earlier traditions, such as Arabic poetry. Although many of these findings emerged after Stone's passing, a contemporary reading of *Approximations to the Object* exposes questions such as: How do the sonnets' representations and forms inherit meaning or content from the meanings or contents of their constituents, even from their absences? How is one supposed to validate and interpret Stone's proposed relationships between iconic content of pictorial representations and the conceptual content he unveils of proposition-like representations? How should one understand Stone's engagement with the history of his time to grasp meanings that remained out of his reach or, perhaps, deliberately omitted? How can the representations of the object-sonnet, even if misguided or biased, evoke parts of the world they represent? While working my way through Stone's tightly argued and incisive treatise, this commentary muses on a very much neglected study of what exists between design and literature, and thus assesses some of the aforementioned questions.

In spite of the fact that William Shakespeare was not the figure who conceived the first sonnet and that its introduction to England in the 16th century is owed to the English politician, ambassador, and lyric poet Thomas Wyatt, it was Shakespeare who accomplished an adaptation of the Petrarchan sonnet to a form that responded to the demands of the English language (the linguistic exigency is the reason there is an evident syllabic difference between the structure and distribution of the verses of the Petrarchan Sonnet and the Shakespearean Sonnet). In this way, I can conclude that both Shakespeare's father and the hand-crafted toy depicted in the toolsheet not only hold a mysterious relation to Francesco Petrarca and Thomas Wyatt, but also make evident that John Shakespeare's craft, and the object itself, were indispensable to the linguistic transformation that William Shakespeare would later effectuate—a transformation initiated from design. Despite a lack of accounts regarding John and William Shakespare's relationship, it is common for certain narcissistic parents to project their dreams and ideals onto their children, hoping they will achieve what the parents themselves could not.[7]

41

In an attempt to continue this writing and keep it brief, I will include two additional case studies that Stone brings to the reader's attention. These are the object-citation and the object-footer. For a clear comprehension, while all the objects included in his work and hence expanded in this text, prefigure the form by which the written word, its symbols and structures, are distributed on the page, each case study illustrates a distinct impact of design on literature:

• A provision of verses for poetic purposes in the object-sonnet

• A resource for intertextual and cognitive connection in the object-citation

• A tool that designates the anatomy of a text in the object-footer

---

[7] Freud in *On Narcissism: An Introduction* (1914), describes how certain parents project their unfulfilled desires onto their children, treating them as incarnations for the dreams they have not realized. He writes: "The child shall fulfill those wishful dreams of the parents which they never carried out... At the most touchy point in the narcissistic system, the immortality of the ego, which is so hard pressed by reality, security is achieved by taking refuge in the child. Parental love (...) is nothing but the parents' narcissism born again." Freud, *On Narcissism: An Introduction* (1914), Standard Edition, vol. XIV, 91.

The Citation & The Object-Citation

I must clarify that Stone is not the first writer of literary, philological or essayistic prose to whom credit is given for having advanced discoveries in design, linguistics, or science. Even though this is not the place to present a comprehensive account of this type of association, and in any case, it is likely that I am not the most suitable person to do so, I cannot help but to mention in this context some relevant examples by way of illustration.

Perhaps it is not mere chance that both the literary theory and the theory of relativity have recurrently lent themselves to this type of comparison. Among the figures cited as alleged precursors to these frameworks in non-scientific writings are personalities as different from each other, such as Lewis Carroll, Novalis, and Maimonides. Without going into further detail, I think it is worth asking what kind of image from the design imaginary and literary activity has led to the assumption that thinkers like the three aforementioned (undoubtedly original, prolific, and well-informed in many fields) could have come up with significant ideas pertinent to disciplines commonly regarded as entirely unrelated.

The forenamed attributions hint at a conception of ideas as eternal and unchanging Platonic archetypes that can be accessed through some mysterious interdisciplinary crack, no matter at what stage in history or in what context of ideas.[1] Thus, confident thinkers may have glimpsed (although it is not known how) some "principle of relativity" before Antoon Lorentz, in 1895, formulated the electrodynamics equations that eventually raised the difficult questions Einstein sought to address with his theory in 1905.[2]

---

[1] The notion of a mysterious interdisciplinary crack relates to Baruch Spinoza's thoughts on certain truths uncovered by the Kabbalists: "A truth that some of the Hebrews appear to have seen as if through a cloud." (Spinoza, *Ethics*, Part II, Proposition 7, *Scholium*)

[2] In a similar vein, Alberto G. Rojo explains in Borges and Quantum Mechanics that Borges unknowingly proposes in his story titled *The Garden of the Forking Paths* a solution to a still unsolved problem in quantum mechanics. *The Garden...* published in 1941, literally anticipates Hugh Everett III's doctoral thesis, published in 1957 under the title *Relative State Formulation of Quantum Mechanics* which Bryce DeWitt later popularized as the *Many Worlds Interpretation of*

Setting aside the hybrid worlds and connections between design, literature, and physics and thus the epistemic emergence of such ideas, Stone outlines an essential genealogy for understanding the citation. Upon citing, I have always reflected on its phonic similarity to the word "site" and, likewise, with the planned encounter of a *cita*.[3] However, prior to encountering *Approximations to the Object*, I had stripped myself from such ideas to believe that the citation, and derivatively the quotation, were concepts originally coined in literary theory.

In a slightly more anthropological vein, as evidenced by his previous research in zoology and antiquarianism[4] prior to the development of *Approximations to the Object*, Stone demonstrates that the origin of the citation and hence of quotation marks is explained by what he designates as the object-citation. I will delve into the origin of such an object in the following paragraphs, but must first underscore that its first appearance dates back to 1700 BCE in Lusatian culture. The presence of such an artifact would have been so significant and geographically extensive that versions of it persisted in European societies from the end of the Bronze Age until the early 1500s.

44

Quantum Mechanics. Therein Borges comes up with a thought experiment referring to the architecture of labyrinthine forking paths which precede the first conceptual revolution of quantum mechanics: the loss of the idea of a trajectory in favor of a description in terms of probabilities of trajectories.

[3] Note from the author: *cita* in the Spanish language refers to both a citation and a romantic date; events where two entities meet.

[4] For other acute and stimulating observations on the same topic, see E. Stone "On Fantastic Antiquarianism," in *Prolegomena to Northumberland's Fantastic Wunderkammer* (1829). This intriguing codex, bound together with albino horsehair, presents a series of wooden boxes containing manuscripts, each paired with the antique object it describes. Across the essays, Stone examines relics found in English 17th-century collections that span centuries and territories, primarily acquired through early English antiquarian trade. These include the first substituted helm, discovered on the shores of Delos, known to belong to the Greek *Ship of Theseus*; a burnt manuscript featuring obsolete punctuation symbols (used to demarcate plagiarism, paraphrasing, and sarcasm) found among scattered fragments attributed to Aristophanes of Byzantium; three marble blocks of different sizes that are said to have induced Pythagoras's theorem; one of the most intertextual and illegible books known to exist as a glass flask containing five mixed grams of ashes from the Library of Alexandria; a circular object that shrinks with forgetfulness and expands with recollection; an early manuscript by Miguel de Cervantes rewriting Pierre Menard's *Quixote*; a lead coin used by medieval tinkers as the kilogram before the kilogram; a fragment of red yarn (approximately a meter in length) used by Eratosthenes during his journey around the globe to measure the Earth's circumference; among others.

By the end of that century, large parts of Europe, particularly regions that would become Germany and England, experienced notable religious transformations that led to their separation from the Roman Catholic Church and the establishment of new, independent ties between several states, principalities, and free cities. The introduction of the printing press to England in 1476 by William Caxton, first developed in Mainz, Germany, by Johannes Gutenberg, epitomizes the mercantile cultural networks of the time and the major circulation of ideas.

Setting aside the archaic era in which the object emerged, *Approximations to the Object* was written by Stone several centuries later during 19th-century England. This society presented fortuitous conditions for his research, primarily due to the pre-established commercial and intellectual proximity between England and Germany. It was during this period that the author, shaped by studies in antiquarianism and philology, was able to uncover a fascinating parallel in his work through the collection of the 18th-century English physician and antiquarian Richard Mead (1673 - 1754): both the object-citation and an early print of *De Vitis Sophistarum* (1516) by the Greek sophist Flavius Philostratus, each of which played a crucial role in Stone's formulation. Both artifacts, presented a deep historical continuity between material and typographic citation; one material, the other printed.

Stone's encounter with Mead's collection was facilitated by his colleague Joseph von Planta, who was the Principal Librarian (i.e. Director) of the British Museum for the first quarter of the 19th century. Following Mead's demise, the institution acquired a vast assortment of ancient objects collected during his lifetime, including coins, medals, gems, intaglios, statuettes, and other artifacts of Germanic and English provenance.[5] Mead was among the few figures in the 18th century who established cultural exchanges with Germany and other European countries. As a personal physician to Queen Caroline

---

[5] Items specifically tied to literary, epistolary, and scholarly traditions, among them some of the object-citations, were later preserved as part of the Britannic Museum of Letters, an archival subdivision whose access is exclusively provided to Stoneian scholars.

of Great Britain and Sir Isaac Newton, Mead possessed substantial contacts and networks throughout Europe. With respect to his German acquisitions, Stone disregarded a large number of Roman books and medieval coins to focus specifically on the Germanic object-citation, Philostratus' book and other illustrations included in the collection.

In *Towards a Universal History of Antiquarians*, archaeologist Alain Schnapp offers a detailed analysis of how the notion of antiquarianism articulates a relationship between memory and forgetting. These ideas, which Schnapp shares in his text, are crucial to understanding antiquarian practice, its appropriative characteristics and the impetus of Stone's study. I believe the latter sought to demonstrate, through a critical study of the object, the ways in which certain modern disciplines exist within a complex network of thought that, at times, fragments subject from object, format from form, knowledge from conspiracy, materiality from discursivity, nature from culture.

46   A non-negligible aspect initially related to the role of antiquarians, librarians, and currently to museum curators precisely concerns the selection of those objects and formats that culture shall preserve, those deemed worthy of conservation, and those which shall elude the passage of time. It is ultimately this (often arbitrary) choice that consequently influences cultural representation and epistemic belief. On this note, Stone's examination would have been non-existent had this selection not taken place beforehand. Therefore, the collection enables both the possibility of discovery and the perpetuation of arbitrariness. In this spirit, Boris Groys questions in his introduction to *In The Flow*: "Why are certain things privileged, why does society care about them and invest money in their conservation and restoration, while other things are delivered to the destructive power of time and nobody cares about their eventual dissolution and disappearance? (...) The antique Greek statues are not more beautiful than a modern car or airplane" (Groys, *In The Flow*, p.10).

By means of thoroughly examining Mead's collection and its accompanying records, Stone managed to discover that the object of his study hailed from the Polish city of Łęgowo in close proximity to Wągrowiec. As previously mentioned, this device specifically dated to the Late Bronze Age and Early Iron Age, when it was part of Lusatian customs, which extended from Poland, the Czech Republic, and Slovakia to eastern Germany.

Considering its geographical circumstances, Stone deduced that Mead's acquisition occurred during one of his literary trips to Germany during the 18th century, specifically his visit to the Leipzig fair of 1723. It is known that Mead procured several rare books and ancient manuscripts for his private library during these excursions. Hence, the literary nature of these expeditions, the ubiquity of the artifact in Germanic regions, the collected volume, and an illustrative archive of the object certified in the same year as the fair, culminate in the unprecedented designation of the object-citation.

To provide the reader with a comprehensive understanding of his argument, Stone briefly introduces the contents of Flavius Philostratus's *De Vitis Sophistarum* before detailing its origin and printing process. This book is known for being the first printed volume to include the typographic leads that would evolve into modern quotation marks used for citation formulae. The edition examined by Stone was an early proof copy from 1516, printed in Strasbourg, Alsace (then part of the Holy Roman Empire), by the printer Mathias Schürer; notable for its marginal annotations and incosistent colophon, suggesting it may have served as a printer's internal specimen.

The inclusion of such text proves crucial for Stone to posit a correspondence between the symbols imprinted in the book, the object-citation and the illustration (all acquired by Mead), given that the form of the first quotation signs followed the shape of the object and thus forewent the development of the marks employed in modern citation methodologies:

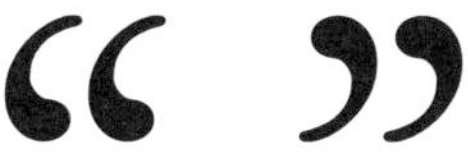

Fig. 1. Modern quotation marks.

In this section, I will also elucidate the illustration acquired by Mead, which the author utilizes to contextualize his study of the object-citation and to substantiate its apparent connection to *De Vitis Sophistarum*. The image was printed using the technique of woodcutting, which involved transferring ink onto paper using a wooden plate, that was inked and pressed. The paper was made of cloth fibers, making it notably resistant and durable. As for the figurative field of the print, it depicts a child holding the artifact in its left hand. It is odd to imagine such an object's existence and even more so in the hands of a child. I must confess that upon confronting this image, I experienced an unsettling experience akin to the frustration of not comprehending, undoubtedly influenced by my way of delving into a fast, extractive, and modern perusal of a text; symptoms of most contemporary readers.

48

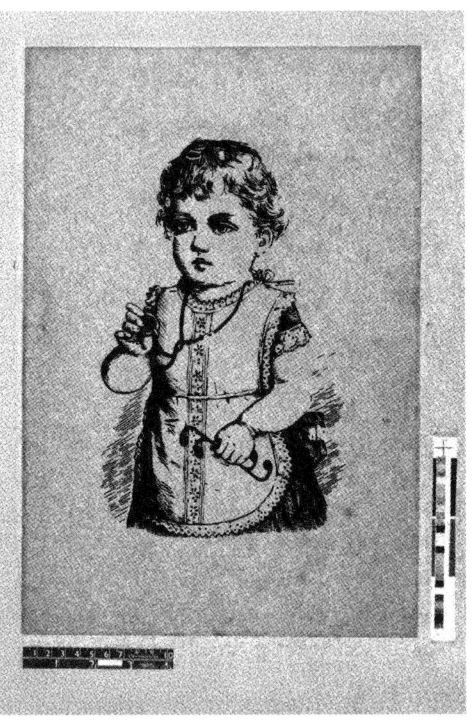

Fig. 2. Xylography of a rattle,
Approximations to the Object, 1827.

With a more compelling diction than the one I shall employ here, Stone explains the inclusion of such an image, describing that "the sign with which Schürer marks the book must be attributed both to the object and the illustration" and further asserts that "the only way to explain the nature of the printed symbol is through its resemblance to the rattles of the time; thus, the object-citation is seen to precede the symbol now formally known as the quotation mark." Through this somewhat arbitrary yet undoubtedly fascinating association, the author demonstrates that the quotation mark originates from the object-citation—an artifact depicted in the printed symbol, preexisting as an object of antiquity, associated with childhood, and comprehensible only through the mechanics of a rattle.

Although this piece appears as early as 1700 BCE, it would have been displaced many centuries later and decontextualized in new European regions, ultimately landing as a cultural fetish in Mead's cabinet of curiosities. While tracing the meandering path of this frail piece across European soil remains highly challenging (due to the dynamic transformations of empires during that time), the resemblance between the shapes acquired by rattles of those centuries, the object-citation and quotation marks is irrefutable.

In the closing remarks of this first analysis, Stone notes:

> The original artifact appeared to be made of terracotta, small in size, hollow inside, and filled with small pebbles. It had an elongated and curved shape and was composed of (what I can only now deduce as) two inverted and mirrored "commas" at each end of the object, which were, in turn, connected by a fragile, and narrow rod. The object seemed to be coated with a protective oil and did not show sharp protrusions. Just as the ears of a pig, for instance, are always connected to its head, the inverted commas on the rattle resemble the lug of an animal. (Stone, 1827, p. 67, §§22–23)

To complement the original woodcut (Fig. 2) from Mead's collection, the author presents additional illustrations belonging to 15th century botanical bestiaries (Fig. 3) that feature the object-citation (also referred to as the "leguminis citationis"). Included as well is a replica of the object (Fig. 4) exhibited at the Britannic Museum of Letters in the late 20th century, which might serve contemporary readers to visualize this study with greater ease.

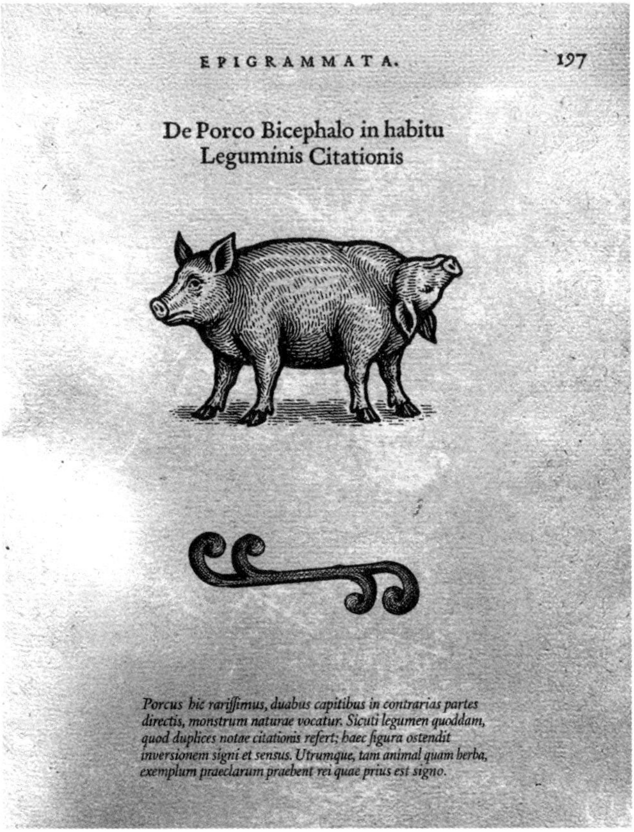

EPIGRAMMATA. 197

De Porco Bicephalo in habitu Leguminis Citationis

Porcus hic rariſſimus, duabus capitibus in contrarias partes directis, monstrum naturae vocatur. Sicuti legumen quoddam, quod duplices notae citationis refert; haec figura ostendit inversionem signi et sensus. Utrumque, tam animal quam herba, exemplum praeclarum praebent rei quae prius est signo.

Fig. 3. *De Porco Bicephalo in habitu Leguminis Citations,* Ashford Antiquarian Library, c. 1634.

The studies on natural sciences by Sir Joseph Banks, an English naturalist and botanist contemporary with Stone, dispelled the author's initial doubts regarding the utility and origin of such an object, asserting that the shape of the ancient rattle was comparable to certain legumes from the *Fabaceae* family and some regional European sea mollusks. It is logical to speculate that this artifact could have evolved in mimesis with nature and that legumes must have been used as infant auditory devices in past millennia before the object-citation's conception and evolution.

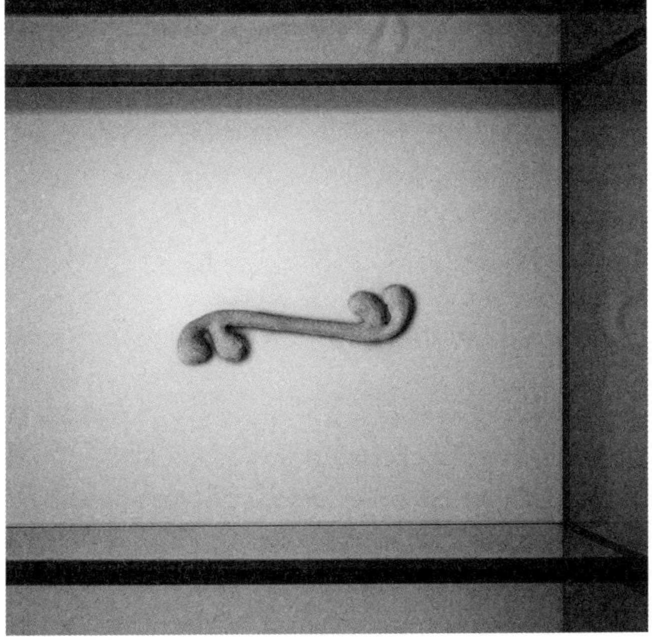

Fig. 4. An object-citation noted as a *Germanic Ornament*,
Britannic Museum of Letters, 1998.

From a botanical perspective, I find it essential to refer to the concepts of phototropism and geotropism in biology (directional responses exhibited by plants in their growth) to explain this literary phenomenon. In geotropism, a plant's movement and orientation follow the Earth's gravitational axis, with the roots growing downward (positive tropism) and the stem growing in the opposite direction (negative tropism). In phototropism, a plant's movement and orientation grow towards (or against) the light. This comparison serves to illustrate that a textual methodology can emerge *from* and be directed *towards* an object, just as the transcendence of the rattle in the Lusatian region presupposes literature's tropism towards objects.

Before concluding his case study, Stone delves into the object-citation's relationship with the aforementioned book. The author firmly attributes the marks deployed in Schürer's print proof as the precursors of modern quotation marks, which evidently take a referential cue from the rattle's silhouette:

> The printed symbol is analogously composed of two inverted and mirrored commas at each end, joined by a thin stroke line. This symbol is located in the left margin of each page outside of the regular type measure and appears at the beginning of each line of a cited passage. (Stone, 1827, p. 73, §§22–23).

We can thus observe how this sign technology gradually evolved into the citation system employed today—the same by which I cite ideas foreign to me in this commentary.

While it is clear that Stone is the one who precisely attributes the origin of the quotation mark in a material and temporal sense, I have decided to include, as part of the genealogy of this sign, Antoine Compagnon's study, as his work has also been influential in the discussion of the symbol. His text, which remains available only in French, titled *La seconde main, ou le travail de la citation* (1979), both challenges and expands ideas concerning the first appearance of the quotation marks, which he (unlike Stone) attributes to the French edition of Petrus Ramus' *Dialecticae Partitiones*, published by André Wechel in Paris in 1555 (thirty-nine years after *De Vitis Sophistarum*):

> Furthermore, since the first French edition of the *Dialecticae* published in 1555 by André Wechel in Paris, all quotes inserted into the text have been distinguished by typography: when in verse, they are printed in italics while the rest of the text is preserved in Roman, and the name of the translator (usually Ronsard) appears at the end of the passage; when in prose, exclusively those of Cicero, a comma is turned back at the level of the verses where the quote begins and ends, accompanied by two commas turned back at the margin of the intermediate lines. These indicators that announce the form of future quotation marks represent a capital innovation. To my knowledge, there is no precedent for such precision in the quotation: beginning

and end unequivocally marked, author and translator designated. (Author's translation.) (Compagnon, Antoine. *La seconde main, ou le travail de la citation*. Paris: Seuil, 1977, p. 246-247.)

En revanche, dès la première édition française de la *Dialectique*, parue en 1555 chez André Wechel à Paris, toutes les citations insérées dans le texte sont distinguées par la typographie: quand elles sont en vers, elles sont imprimées en italique, l'ensemble du texte étant en romain, et le nom du traducteur (le plus souvent Ronsard) figure au bas du passage; quand elles sont en prose, exclusivement celle de Cicéron, une virgule retournée se trouve en marge, à hauteur des lignes où la citation commence et se termine, deux virgules retournées en marge des lignes intermédiaires. Ces indicateurs qui annoncent les futurs guillemets, sous la forme qu'ils prendront au siècle suivant, représentent une innovation capitale. Il n'y a que je sache, pas d'antécédent à une telle précision dans la citation: début et fin repérés sans équivoque, auteur et traducteur désignés. (Paris: Seuil, 1977, p. 246-247.)

53

While Stone does acknowledge the typographic innovations in *Dialecticae Partitiones*, he references them only as a consequence of the earlier appearance of the object-citation marks in Schürer's *De Vitis Sophistarum*, which he considers the first formal citation prototype to mirror this referential device.

Continuing the design historiography of the quotation mark, I will present the visual aids referenced by Stone to depict the representation of the object and its abstract formalization. These resources provide valuable perspectives on the object-citation as a precedent visual reference for the contemporary quotation mark.

[See next spread]

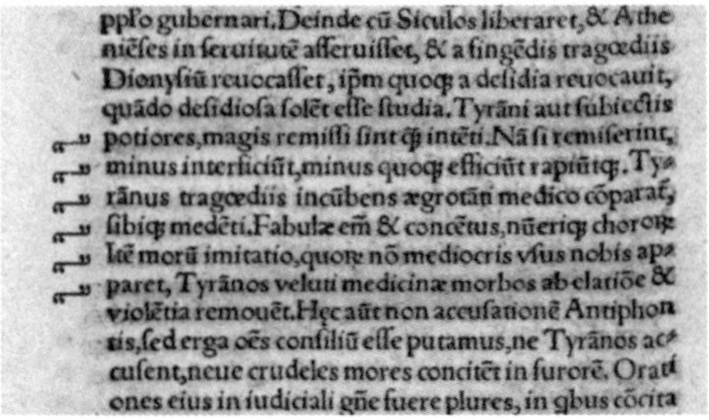

ppło gubernari.Deinde cũ Siculos liberaret,& Athe
nieſes in ſeruitutẽ aſſeruiſſet,& a fingẽdis tragœdiis
Dionyſiũ reuocaſſet,ipm quoqʒ a deſidia reuocauit,
quãdo deſidioſa ſolẽt eſſe ſtudia.Tyrãni aut ſubiectiis
potiores,magis remiſſi ſint qʒ intẽti.Nã ſi remiſerint,
minus interficiũt,minus quoqʒ efficiũt rapiũtqʒ.Ty
rãnus tragœdiis incũbens ægrotãti medico cõparaf,
ſibiqʒ medẽti.Fabulæ em̃ & concẽtus,nũeriqʒ choroʒ̃
lẽ morũ imitatio,quoʒ̃ nõ mediocris vſus nobis ap
paret,Tyrãnos veluti medicinæ morbos ab elatiõe &
violẽtia remouẽt.Hęc aũt non accuſatiõe Antiphon
tis,ſed erga oẽs conſiliũ eſſe putamus,ne Tyrãnos ac
cuſent,neue crudeles mores concitẽt in furorẽ.Orati
ones eius in iudiciali gñe fuere plures,in qbus cõcita

Fig. 5. Mathias Schürer's print of *De Vitis Sophistarum*
by Flavius Philostratus, Germany, 1516. Example of
object-citation marks on the left margin of page 29.

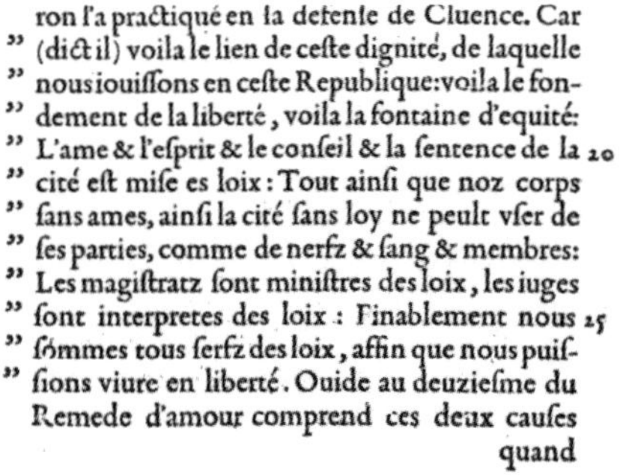

ron l'a practiqué en la defenſe de Cluence. Car
" (dict il) voila le lien de ceſte dignité, de laquelle
" nous iouiſſons en ceſte Republique: voila le fon-
" dement de la liberté , voila la fontaine d'equité:
" L'ame & l'eſprit & le conſeil & la ſentence de la 20
" cité eſt miſe es loix : Tout ainſi que noz corps
" ſans ames, ainſi la cité ſans loy ne peult vſer de
" ſes parties, comme de nerfz & ſang & membres:
" Les magiſtratz ſont miniſtres des loix, les iuges
" ſont interpretes des loix : Finablement nous 15
" ſõmmes tous ſerfz des loix, affin que nous puiſ-
" ſions viure en liberté . Ouide au deuzieſme du
Remede d'amour comprend ces deux cauſes
quand

Fig. 6. *Dialecticae partitiones*, French edition, by
Petrus Ramus, published in Paris in 1555. Example of
early quotation marks on the left margin of page 10.

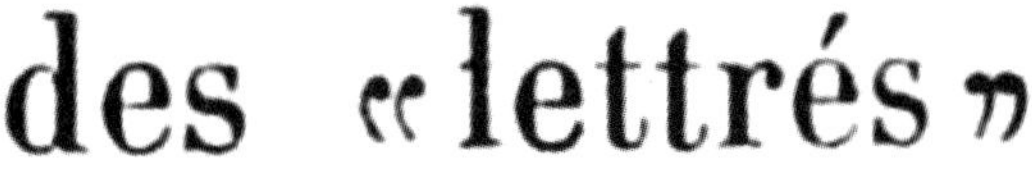

des «lettrés»

Fig. 7. Guillemets produced by the Imprimerie
Nationale, featured in *Bulletin Typographique des Possessions
Extérieures*, No. 302 (May 1802), showing the usage of paired
marks, opening and closing, at the level of lower case letters.

Following this succession of images—their representations and similarities—it is vital to highlight that it is not only the form of the citation that is oriented towards the object but also its function.

From an anthropological perspective, the early presence and transcendence of the rattle in the Lusatian region expose the relationship between literature and objects. It is inevitable for me to ponder that, just as a citation draws the reader's attention to another text, a rattle draws the listener's attention through sound. Interestingly, such an artifact provides early auditory and tactile stimulation for infants. The soft sounds, such as the rustling seeds of a leaf, enable a child to perform associative processes, forming a relationship between a sound and the object that produces it. By shaking a rattle, a child begins to cognitively associate sounds with objects, which makes this event inherently a citational act. In the search for that which emits sound, the coordination of the auditory and visual senses produces an encounter with meaning.[6]

In this manner, the repetitive character of the sounds that arise from shaking a rattle prefigures the "refrain" (as referred to by Gilles Deleuze and Félix Guattari), the iteration, and the commitment to what returns, which characterizes citation as a literary resource. As such, a rattle is a machine for reiterating and repeating, for bringing back.[7]

55

---

[6] The object-citation symbol has often been confused with the eighth note or the quarter note due to their graphic resemblance. While both of these musical notes are used to indicate duration, and the object-citation sign could be seen to demarcate a beginning and an ending, it may be more fitting to relate it to the way certain graphemes, such as the single letter "o," readily prompt their corresponding phoneme /o/, which simultaneously requires the speaker to round their lips into a circular "o" shape to effectively produce the sound. It is thus natural to associate a shape with a sound, as shown by the so-called "bouba-kiki effect" (Ramachandran & Hubbard 2001)—a non-arbitrary synesthetic connection between the shape of an image and the sound of the associated word. Martino Manca, an Italian philosopher, mentions this effect in his paper *Sense Without (Semantic) Meaning? The Case of Asemic Writing*.

[7] "A child in the dark, gripped with fear, comforts himself by singing under his breath. He walks and halts to his song. Lost, he takes shelter, or orients himself with his little song as best he can. The song is like a rough sketch of a calming and stabilizing, calm and stable, center in the heart of chaos. Perhaps the child skips as he sings, hastens or slows his pace. But the song itself is already a skip: it jumps from chaos to the beginnings of order in chaos and is in danger of breaking apart at any moment." Gilles Deleuze and Félix Guattari, *A Thousand Plateaus: Capitalism and Schizophrenia* (Minneapolis: University of Minnesota Press, 1987), 310.

To resume the study, Stone refers to the rattle and the object-citation as one, two sides of the same coin. Both have preceded the emergence of citation and are essential for deciphering the totality of the object's being and functioning. Given that the appearance of the "quotation marks" shares its form with the rattle, the senses instigated by such an object are likely to have influenced Mathias Schürer's imagination and material sensibility. Although there is no specific evidence of the presence of this artifact in Schürer's childhood, these infantile objects were common and customary among European aristocratic families of the time. As such, the rattles, and even more astonishingly, the impression of Mathias Schürer's *De Vitis Sophistarum* by Flavius Philostratus, printed in Germany in 1516, provide sufficient evidence to demonstrate how the object became abstracted into the sign.

Such a case's cognitive and poetic aspects are related to synesthesia as a rhetorical figure in literature. One could reason that Mathias Schürer's print was undoubtedly conditioned by his early interaction with a rattle of the time, inducing a potential synesthetic experience. The printer's receptivity to the form and function of the object would have occurred with such acute sensitivity that he could transcend the very form and function of the rattle. In some way, personalities like Schürer or Shakespeare are precisely what fascinate Stone, as they expose how, even under the jurisdiction of a presupposed and established form and function, objects have, beyond their practical use, a pre-semiotic dimension that is primarily narrative and imaginary—one that is paradoxically triggered when they are displaced and perceived outside of their primitive context; the only space where unequivocal psychological receptivity may occur. Jean Baudrillard develops a similar argument in *The System of Objects*, and the inclusion of this idea serves to expand Stone's study. Baudrillard expresses in a comparable way that objects "are the reflection of a whole view of the world according to which each being is a vessel of inwardness" and that "relations between beings are transcendent correlations of substances; thus the house itself is the symbolic equivalent of the human body, whose potent organic schema is later generalized into an ideal design for the integration of social structures." (Baudrillard, 1996, p. 28)

In the case studies of *Approximations to the Object,* Stone engages in a reading of things, an exercise that centuries later Baudrillard perceives as lost. Both authors seem to be interested in the material and mental structures (which in Stone's view generate meaning through their entanglement with objects) that overlap and contradict the functional structures of the world: the cultural, infra-, or transcultural systems on which meaning or lived every-dayness, are based. Baudrillard further posits that:

> The technological plane is an abstraction: in ordinary life, we are practically unconscious of the technological reality of objects (...) Thus, with meaning and value deriving from the hereditary trans-mission of substances under the jurisdiction of form, the world is experienced as given (as it always is in the unconscious and in childhood), and the task is to reveal and perpetuate it. So, too, with the form perfectly circumscribing the object, a portion of nature is included therein, just as in the case of the human body: the object in this view is essentially anthropomorphic. (Baudrillard, 1996, p. 5)

57

The displacement of the sign and the technology that allows for such displace-ment (a map, a boat, a backpack, a mercantile network, among others) given in certain economic, social, and cultural conditions, allows for a thing's permutation of meaning. It is worth noting that similar rattles (but not iden-tical) were also present in ancient Egypt and Siberia during the same period, and are difficult to locate today. Their widespread geographic presence accentuates the fundamental human need for this artifact and its multi-plicity across different cultures and eras. Returning to the idea that meaning emerges through displacement, one might speculate that, had the printing press appeared in a different region or during a different time, it is entirely plausible that the graphic sign of the quotation mark might have responded instead to other culturally distinct rattle formations across those latitudes and epochs. In this spirit, Jun'ichirō Tanizaki's *In Praise of Shadows* muses on how the hypothetical appearance of the pen would have looked like had it been invented in Japan.   [See next spread]

To take a trivial example near at hand: I wrote a magazine article recently comparing the writing brush with the fountain pen, and in the course of it, I remarked that if the device had been invented by the ancient Chinese or Japanese, it would surely have had a tufted end like our writing brush. The ink would not have been this bluish color but rather black, something like India ink, and it would have been made to seep down from the handle into the brush. And since we would have then found it inconvenient to write on Western paper, something near Japanese paper—even under mass production, if you will—would have been most in demand. Foreign ink and pen would not be as popular as they are; the talk of discarding our system of writing for Roman letters would be less noisy; people would still feel an affection for the old system. But more than that, our thought and our literature might not be imitating the West as they are, but might have pushed forward into new regions quite on their own. An insignificant little piece of writing equipment, when one thinks of it, has had a vast, almost boundless, influence on our culture. But I know as well as anyone that these are the empty dreams of a novelist, and that having come this far we cannot turn back. I know that I am only grumbling to myself and demanding the impossible. (Tanizaki, 1977, p. 7)

In essence, the tension between reality and representation is made evident in this case study. Abstraction is forgetfulness and ease, rolling on a tacit underlying logic that we often disregard, a reason and an intuition that are harnessed yet appeased, to become the nightmare itself. Abstraction is thus the generation of models of the real without a specific origin or reality (or rather, one too deeply sedimented). The object-citation no longer precedes the marks nor does it survive them in contemporary culture. We could suppose that such an object has undoubtedly proven to precede the citation, but only insofar as it has surpassed its meaning through permutations, subjectivities, and variable uses. What preceded the sign in the past is dissolved in the abstraction of the present. Hereby, Baudrillard goes one step further to declare that the information and communication technologies of the late 20th century provoke such confusion between what is real and what is represented that it has become increasingly laborious to distinguish them. It would seem, then, that differentiating between reality and representation no longer makes sense.

By no means do I intend to become a source of anxiety or confusion, but this tension is what induced me to materially reproduce the objects included in this commentary as an attempt to blend the real and the represented.[8]

The boundaries between reality and representation have also been addressed through studies of spatial perception and cognition by child psychologists like Jean Piaget and Donald Winnicott. For instance, the latter pediatrician studied play as an essential factor of maturation, describing how children relate to the outside world of objects and spaces in a very fluid and labile way.

In discussing the value of play, interaction, and discovery, Winnicott introduces the concept of "transitional objects," which are so entangled in the imagination of the beholder that they neither fully exist as external things nor are entirely part of the self. (Some of these involve particularly soft objects, such as blankets or stuffed animals, which infants rely on during moments of separation from the mother.) In this manner, he argues that the realm of play must remain far from empiricist reductionism, such as the question: "Did you find that (in the world), or did you make it up?" as it would negate the internal order of the child's world—one that shall remain forever untranslatable and beyond the grasp of reason. Thus, to completely distinguish an external, a priori "real world" from one that is constructed and participatory would not only negate imagination, but also contradict the innate capacity of human beings to structure reciprocal relationships with their environment; for the world cannot be wholly reduced to either external reality or internal fantasy, but instead occupies an intermediate realm—something simultaneously made-up, inferred, imagined, and encountered.

59

---

[8] The process of manufacturing and reproducing such objects and their relationship with writing are discussed, as an appendix to the commentary, in the epilogue of this work.

Respectively, Borges and Carroll have explored the interpretation of reality in their stories. In Borges' *On Exactitude in Science*, a map becomes so large that it covers the territory it represents, rendering it useless; and in Carroll's *Sylvie and Bruno* (from which Borges builds), a professor proudly announces the development of a map "on the scale of a mile to the mile." In this sense, while these stories expose how the drive to perfectly represent reality is self-defeating (as map and territory collapse into one another), Baudrillard goes further, claiming that models of reality give rise to the hyperreal, where the map no longer precedes the territory, nor survives it. Winnicott, conversely, highlights the futility of differentiating between the two or determining which holds precedence. Hence, deciphering whether something belongs to nature or artifice appears ultimately as a flawed inquiry, one that presumes reality and imagination, world and mind, as mutually exclusive. But as the examples of literary design objects or maps might suggest, such entities transcend division: they are neither fully found nor fully invented, but rather emerge from an entanglement within domains and the interactions that shape them.

60

Thus, while Winnicott is concerned with how the self forms through encounters with the phenomenal world, and Baudrillard with the dissolution of difference within contemporary culture and its systems of production, both acknowledge the blending of artifice and found nature; where invention and discovery intertwine to assemble reality as a thoroughly mediated product.

In the same spirit, for Stone, reality is not something external and "given" for our apprehension, but it is constituted through our participation with things: objects, images, values, codes, maps, and so forth. "What we observe is never nature in itself," he writes "but nature constrained by the method of our understanding, articulated through the grammar of our inquiry. Yet not all things enter this grammar evenly." Some objects, he contends, precede our frameworks of sense. Their material forms prefigure meaning, in so far as our interactions enclose them within the metaphysics of language. (Some reflections in the preceding paragraphs draw upon James Corner's thoughts in his thought-provoking essay *The Agency of Mapping* published in 1999.)

The Footer & The Object-Footer

The abhorrent object-footer observes the passage of a technological
system to a cultural system in which the object is the protagonist
and responds to its own functions, even if it subverts its prior utility,
or is in contradiction with its original technical system.
—Edmund Stone, *Approximations to the Object*

With the aforecited quotation, Stone opens the present section, which is somewhat obscure and peculiar if one is able to understand the historical relationship between the object-footer and the footnote, which explains the origin of this textual methodology and the anatomical distribution of the modern text.

At the beginning of the case study, the author reminds the reader that "a footnote is an intervention in a text at its bottom margin." Ironically, the history of the footnote can be narrated through a succession of footnotes, and while Stone considers Saint Bede, a Benedictine monk from the 8th century, to be its creator, there is still no consensus regarding its origins.

In *The Devil's Details: A History of Footnotes*, Chuck Zerby asserts that its introduction happened several centuries later with the British painter and printer Richard Jugge. Conversely, *The Footnote: A Curious History*, by Anthony Grafton, discusses other names, such as the father of scientific historiography, Leopold von Ranke, the philologists Ulrich von Wilamowitz-Möllendorff and Jacob Bernays, the English historian Richard White of Basingstoke, and the German Jesuit Athanasius Kircher. Conceptually, Umberto Eco, in *How to Write a Thesis*, explains the differences between quotation, paraphrasing, and plagiarism. One of the uses he details for the footnote is to "pay debts." Other writers like Georges Perec advocate that the path of art (literature) is in the citation, in the author's ability to appropriate the thoughts of those who came before them.[1]

---

[1] These references have been instrumental in assembling a conceptual framework through which to contextualize Stone's own deployment of the object-footer.

Prior to delving into the object-footer analysis, it is worth recalling Nietzsche's proposal in *On the Genealogy of Morals*: that, in order to create a memory of words, humans had to resort to systems of cruelty that inscribed themselves upon the body, leaving scars as a promise. He writes, "When man decided he had to make a memory for himself, it never happened without blood, torments and sacrifices: the most horrifying sacrifices and forfeits (the sacrifice of the first-born belongs here), the most disgusting mutilations (for example, castration), the cruelest rituals of all religious cults (and all religions are, at their most fundamental, systems of cruelty)—all this has its origin in that particular instinct which discovered that pain was the most powerful aid to mnemonics."

These philosophical inheritances aid in my analysis of what Stone refers to as a "historical object-schematic concatenation of bloody events towards the footnote" during the time of Saint Bede, also known as the Venerable Bede or Beda. Stone attributes to Bede the invention of the footnote, and it is through the object-footer that he is able to credit this capital innovation. Bede was an English monk at the monastery of Saint Peter in the Kingdom of Northumbria of the Angles (currently Monkwearmouth-Jarrow Abbey in Tyne and Wear, England). It is worth noting that he was one of the greatest teachers and writers of the Early Middle Ages, and many historians consider him the most important scholar of antiquity between the death of Pope Gregory I in 604 and the coronation of Charlemagne in 800.

In *Approximations to the Object*, Stone emphasizes the importance of Saint Bede in the genesis of the footer (and by extension, the footnote), an event that Stone attributes to his work *Historia ecclesiastica gentis Anglorum*. This text is considered one of the first to include annotations, notes, or writings in the bottom margin of a text. In his manuscript, Saint Bede utilized footnotes to clarify the content of the main text and cite sources. This novel intervention allowed readers to access additional information without interrupting the reading of the main text. Stone remarks that, as a renowned piece of English literature, the work was a significant contribution to England's history, and he laments the deplorable condition of the manuscript under his inquiry.

To delve further into this commentary and position it in the 21ˢᵗ century, I have inquired Stone's inclusion of the ancient writing of the Anglo-Saxon theologian. An understanding of such must ponder its positionality as a text of medieval England, a society in which the first use of a footnote system would have been congruent with its systems of control, power, punishment, the illusion of an author,[2] and a presumed "unequivocal" episteme. Eco's idea of paying debts[3] concerning the footnote is illustrative in understanding the Anglo-Saxon legal system of the Middle Ages, the clinical context, and the *modus operandi* for accusing and eradicating heresy in the societies of the time.

The 8ᵗʰ century in England was characterized, among many things, by an Anglo-Saxon system of coercion based on an economy of punishment: the punished body, dismembered, amputated, its flesh symbolically marked, exposed, offered as a spectacle. Punishments were largely proportional to the offense and in accordance with the social status of the offender and victim. In turn, amputation became a craft, a cure, a treatment, and a form of chastisement. It is certain that by the mid-medieval period, a competent surgeon could complete the amputation of a leg in less than five minutes from the

---

[2] Foucault reasserts the reliability of authorship in the middle ages by stating "Texts, however, that we now call 'scientific' (dealing with cosmology and the heavens, medicine or illness, the natural sciences or geography) were only considered truthful during the Middle Ages if the name of the author was indicated." and continues to explain: "It would be as false to seek the author in relation to the actual writer as to the fictional narrator; the 'author- function' arises out of their scission—in the division and distance of the two. (...) The 'author-function' is tied to the legal and institutional systems that circumscribe, determine, and articulate the realm of discourses; it does not operate in a uniform manner in all discourses, at all times, and in any given culture; it is not defined by the spontaneous attribution of a text to its creator, but through a series of precise and complex procedures; it does not refer, purely and simply, to an actual individual insofar as it simultaneously gives rise to a variety of egos and to a series of subjective positions that individuals of any class may come to occupy." Michel Foucault, "What Is an Author?" in *Textual Strategies: Perspectives in Post-Structuralist Criticism*, edited by Josué V. Harari (Ithaca: Cornell University Press, 1979), 149.

[3] On this note, to preempt any accusations of academic embezzlement, I shall repay my debt to Umberto Eco by affirming that he, in fact, affirms: "Use notes to pay your debts. Citing a book from which you copied a sentence is paying a debt. Citing an author whose ideas or information you used is paying a debt. Sometimes, though, you must also pay debts that are more difficult to document. It is a good rule of academic honesty to mention in a note that, for example, a series of original ideas in your text could not have been born without inspiration from a particular work, or from a private conversation with a scholar." Umberto Eco, *How to Write a Thesis*, trans. Caterina Mongiat Farina and Geoff Farina (Cambridge, MA: MIT Press, 2015), 132.

initial surgical incision. The leg was removed in less than a minute, and the remaining time was allocated to bleeding control. Medieval surgeons of the time restored the practice of using ligatures on blood vessels in some cases, which the ancient Greeks had practiced centuries earlier. (Presumably, Greek knowledge has continually crossed borders, cultures, and centuries.)

Setting aside the clinical details, the locus of both my interest and Stone's research resides in the object-footer (artifact precedent to the footer), the life of the scholar Edward Mervin Foote, and the epidemiological and cultural context of the time. Through a meticulous and deliberately recorded analysis, Stone explains what would be later elucidated by both Jacques Derrida and Mark Fisher: the notion of an aura that haunts us, and more precisely, the concept of *hauntology*; the spectral character of past ideologies (embodied in objects) whose ontological ambiguity persists in the present as intangible ghosts of the contemporary world. Stone radicates this argument in the design object as a "premonitory agent whose permanence endures in the crumbling of the future into the past, perpetually in the present."

Contemporarily, the philosopher and critic Mark Fisher has referred to *hauntology* as the concept that captures "the fact that nothing enjoys a positive existence. Everything that exists is possible only on the basis of a series of absences that precede it, surround it, and enable it to possess consistency and intelligibility." Similarly, the philosopher Martin Hägglund defined this concept as opposed to the traditional ontology that reflects being qua identical self-presence, explaining that what is of relevance about the figure of the specter is that it cannot be fully present: it is not a being in itself but points to a relationship with what is no longer or with what is not yet.[4]

It is through the case of the object-footer that Stone demonstrates the (somewhat spectral) relationship between body, object, name, and text, primarily

---

[4] Courtney Smith offers a compelling essay on the relationship between ghosts and amputation, titled *The Logic of Phantom Semantics*. Therein the artist explores the concepts of the "phantom limb" and "phantom pain." Much like the specter of past ideologies that lingers in objects, these metaphorical expressions articulate a form of pain that reasserts in an absence.

how the primitive unintelligibility of an object persists and displaces itself within consciousness, when it attempts to be captured through abstract reasoning, without losing its material and bodily dimension altogether. Essentially, when discourse tries to fix an object, something is lost from the raw material it manipulates.

The biography of Edward Mervin Foote is circumstantial to the exploration that I present in this commentary, one that concerns design and literature, particularly object and text. Nonetheless, Stone expresses genuine interest in Mervin Foote, as he was a contemporary of Bede and is believed to be the fabricator of the object-footer. Thus, this figure is essential for situating the development of the artifact and tracing a lineage towards the footnote in medieval England. While many cultures have carried out the practice of amputation since antiquity, the work of Mervin Foote excelled as it marked the beginning of a textual phenomenon.

According to tradition, Edward Mervin Foote, also known as Saint Mervin Foote or Saint Foote, was a 7th-century English saint and hermit known for his advancements in bellic and medical technologies around the year 640 in the region of Kent, southeastern England. Stone recounts how he built the first mutilator—alternatively, the object-footer—during his time as a hermit in *Beorhtel's Wood*, within the parish of Folkestone. The specific reason for the development of such technology remains undetermined to this day, whether it was to exert power, mutilate heretics, or improve quality of life in the face of diseases prevalent during that period. Despite the initial purpose remaining unverified, Mervin Foote became a saint to the region's people due to his significant impact on the health of medieval English populations. After his death in 693, his cult rapidly spread throughout England, and he was formally canonized in 1189 during the pontificate of Pope Clement III.

By the time of Stone's writing, Mervin Foote was already commemorated on the Feast of Saint Foote, celebrated on March 16 by the Catholic Church and on March 24 by the Anglican Church. (With a twist of fate, the transition from medieval religious calendars to our own has undergone the same abstraction as many of these literary occurrences. Similarly, we often forget the very figures or events we are meant to commemorate.)

Following Stone's perspective, the development of such an artifact would have been initially destined for foot mutilation, to exercise punishment, and to treat diseases such as gangrene and leprosy in the face of poor hygiene and wars, characteristic of the infections and plagues of medieval times. Both the object-footer and the whip (or Roman flagellum) embody the penal systems of the Middle Ages, and just as the processions of flagellants reached such a degree of popularity in Spain that they even appear in Miguel de Cervantes' *Don Quixote*, the object-footer proves central in Stone's literature and for the comprehension of the anatomical distribution of the modern text:

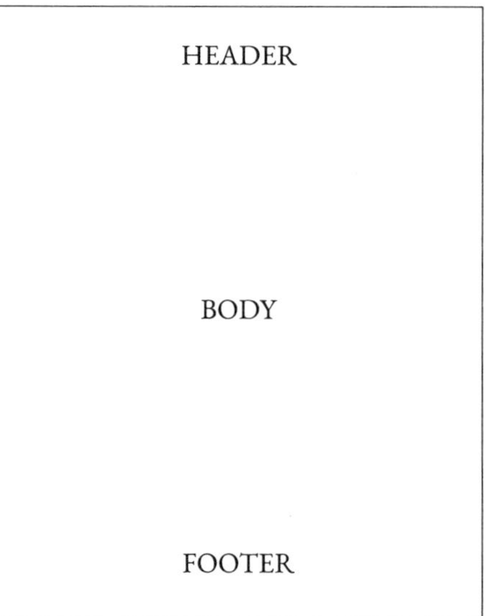

Fig. 1. Distribution of a modern text.

Unlike fines, such physical punishments reaffirmed themselves over the body, much as words reaffirm themselves over a page. Design in this context becomes an instrument and intermediary between body and ideology, the punished and the punisher. This intervention activates a system of coercion and deprivation, obligations and prohibitions. Centuries later, the exemplary mechanics of design punishment[5] would change its gears, abstracting itself from physical suffering, the pain of the body itself, to become hidden in its bones, beneath its living skin, evolving to be the most concealed aspect of the designed penal procedure. The latter point is notably studied by Michel Foucault in *Discipline and Punish*, exemplified in the Panopticon structure devised by the English mechanical engineer and naval architect Samuel Bentham, a model also implicit in contemporary digital surveillance.

Stone's acumen in structuring the relationship between language (word) and object (mutilator) from a cultural and technological perspective is exceptional. The inclusion of the "foot" in the appellation of the object is essential to establishing its future semiotic interplay. Even more fascinating is the name's transcendence amidst the technē's continual evolution.[6] The latter point is apparent in the object-footer, which, despite its mysterious origins, establishes a singular sense or function in the penal and surgical realm (that of mutilation) and yet is capable of reconstituting its meaning upon another use. The interference of language ("foot") in its designation permitted its diffusion into another practical system; that of writing. In this plane, the intrusion of the word obliterates the original object, instead transposing it into a novel sense, that of structuring a text. This dynamic reveals the fascinating linguistic play between the system of objects and that of words (as seen

---

[5] Paola Antonelli and Jamer Hunt explore in *Design and Violence* the complex impact of design on the built environment and on everyday life, as well as on the forms of violence in contemporary society. (Antonelli Paola, and Jamer Hunt. *Design and Violence*. Museum of Modern Art, 2013).

[6] Martin Heidegger explains in *The Question Concerning Technology* (1954) that the word "technology" is derived from the Greek *technikon*, which is related to the word *technē*. In the sense of "technique," *technē* refers to both manufacturing (the techniques of printers, for example) and to the arts (the techniques of poets and graphic designers). *Technē* is part of *poiesis*. Furthermore he posits that in Greek thought from Plato on, the word is used in connection with the word episteme. *Technē*, Heidegger concludes "does not lie at all in making and manipulating nor in the using of means, but rather in the revealing." Such a view opens the possibility of interpreting historical tools or designed literary objects not simply as instruments, but as forms through which something is revealed.

in graphemes and phonemes entangled with artifacts) capable of producing novel semantic meaning and domain shifts.

We thus see how text is fragmented and mutilated, its order structured around the body. Therefore, we know not the thing in itself, but only in relation to another. We are unable to enunciate without referring, and upon invoking the word footer, the body immediately transposes the text into another body, and we surrender once again to a game of references: things that refer to others, and even, things that when referring, refer to themselves.[7]

Such interference of language in the technical realm, as an orderly nomenclature, influenced the work of St. Bede, when designating the bottom margin of his texts as "footers." Thus, the text took on attributes analogous to the anatomy of the human body, which were fundamental elements already evidenced in the eponymous piece produced by Mervin Foote.

Stone jocularly reiterates that "St. Bede, in a manner not unlike, discharged his intellectual debts through footnotes, even as heretics did make amends for their transgressions through the grievous mutilation of their own feet." This association for settling intellectual debts is ingenious for explaining the role of the footnote and its indebted relationship to the object-footer; the latter being a device that does not merely serve as a precedent to anatomical textuality but altogether as a mechanism of debt, a prosthesis of guilt, and a visible concession to epistemic authority.

------

[7] Aristotle's critique of Plato's *Theory of Forms*, known as the *Third Man Argument*, illustrates how identity is never self-contained but always dependent on another layer of reference. If individual *men* are explained by the archetypal "Man," then the relation between them necessitates yet another *form* to account for their commonality, leading to an infinite regress. Similarly, the anatomical fragmentation of the text and thus the imposed order of header-body-footer suggest that once again this is not casual but materially relational, always referring to something beyond itself. Just as we do not know "the thing" but only "the thing in relation to another thing," Aristotle reveals that we do not grasp "Man" as an absolute entity but only through an endless chain of references. Hence, if there is to be something such as *Man*, an archetype for the many *men*, one would have to postulate another archetype to include them all, and then a fourth, and so on... This recursive structure underscores the tension between enunciating, defining and referring, as every utterance draws its meaning from an ever-expanding network of associations... We are left wondering, would there be a *footer* without a *foot*? A *Man* without *men*?

In reference to this last point, it is Foucault who argues centuries later in *What is an Author?* that the author is "an ideological figure by which one marks the manner in which we fear the proliferation of meaning." He observes that, for modernity, the author is regarded as "the genial creator of a work in which he deposits, with infinite wealth and generosity, an inexhaustible world of significations." Yet this supposed genius, Foucault contends, masks a deeper function: not the abundant generation of ideas, but the author's role as an anchor, a mechanism by which society sustains a structure of control over meaning and knowledge. (Foucault, 1979, p. 149)

Stone anticipates this logic in his reflections on the object-footer, wherein authorship concerns not only the act of writing but also the act of sinning; the author is not merely the inventor of ideas, but their judge and executioner. In this way, the footnote in medieval England introduced a device for textual authority and legitimacy, grounded in the author's exposition of his sources, yet it simultaneously undermined that authority by allowing the reader to disregard them and embark on a divergent journey. It appears, therefore, that beyond its material object, the object-footer, and consecutively, the footnote, is transgression and control, discipline and release. Author and reader, mythology and reality, mutilator and heretic are the dichotomies of our societies of control, which overlap to reflect ourselves in our artifacts and imprison us through the unintelligible authority of the past over the present.

While acknowledging Stone's prophetic value, *Approximations to the Object* still operates in this authoritative logic. His work constantly strives to attribute and name, to find an origin, a fixed truth. Thus, I must express my disagreement with the underlying logic of an author to whom we are endowed. If there is to be a leading author in these case studies, I postulate it be the objects themselves. However, the very liveliness of their being is imbued in an inanimate facade. Thus, these usually remain unrecognizable as epistemic agents, forms ineffable to the identity, name, or features of a genius. Hence, I question: In what ways can we envisage the meaning manifesting through objects and fulfill our obligations towards them?

Included herein are the sources referenced in Stone's analysis: a fragmentary manuscript bearing a footer inscription in its lower margin, attributed to St. Bede (Fig. 2), an illustration of a medieval amputation procedure (Fig. 3), and a print depicting Mervin Foote holding such an artifact (Fig. 4). (An additional image of the object-footer is also provided for a thorough analysis.)

70

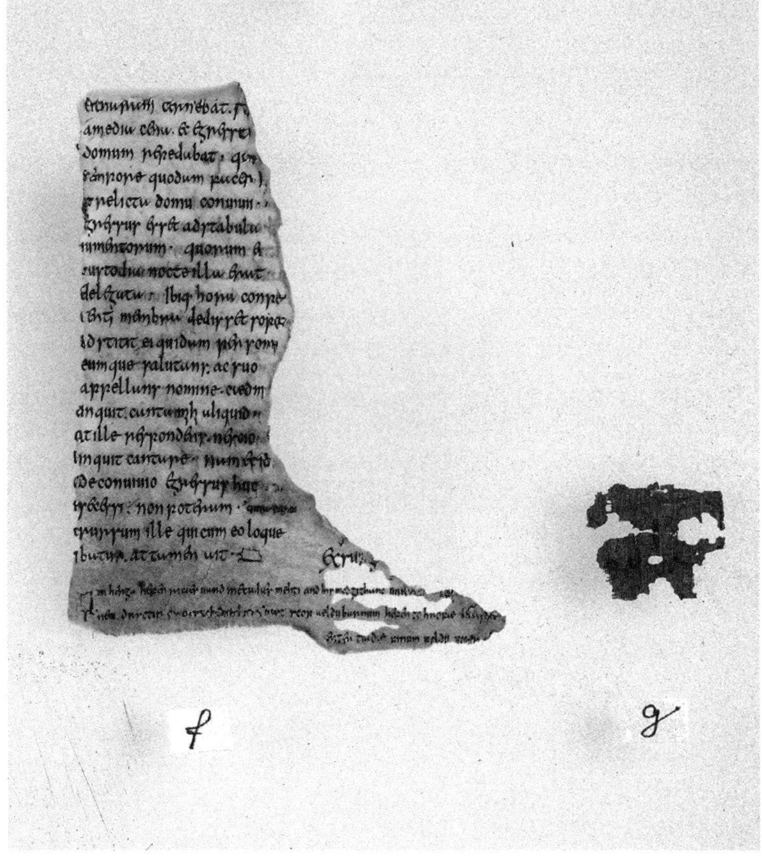

Fig. 2. Fragmentary manuscript of Bede's
Ecclesiastical History of the English People, c. 731 CE.

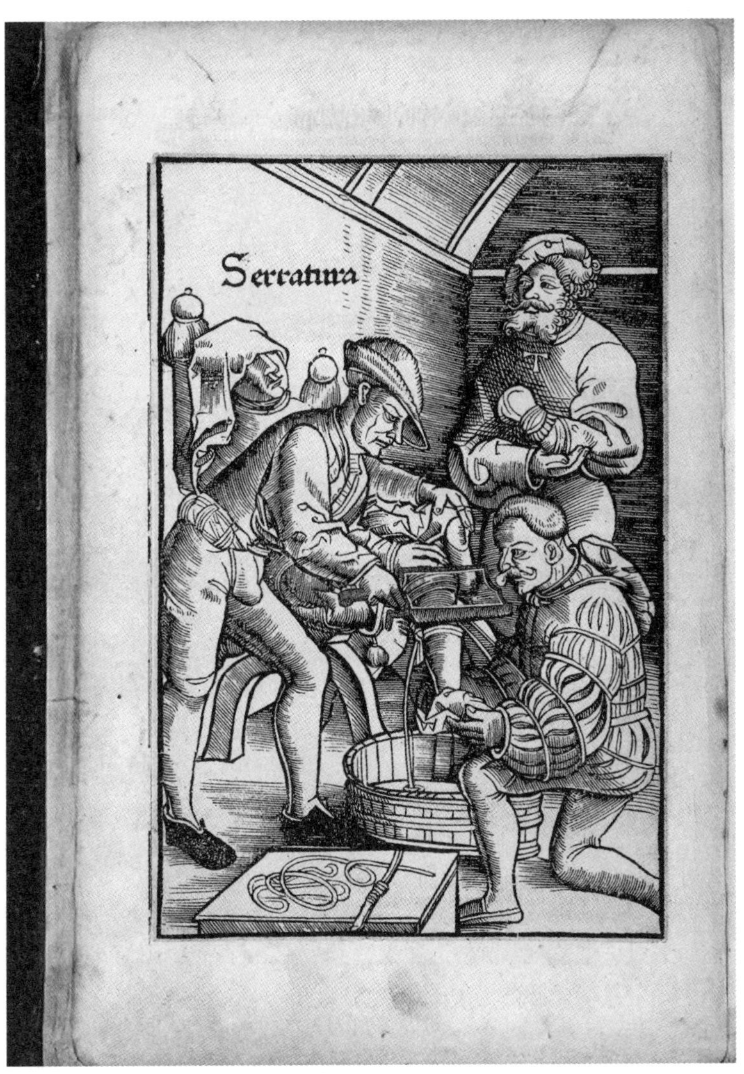

Fig. 3. *The Field Book of Surgery*
by Scheel-Hans de Hans von Gersdorf, Amsterdam, c. 1593.

72

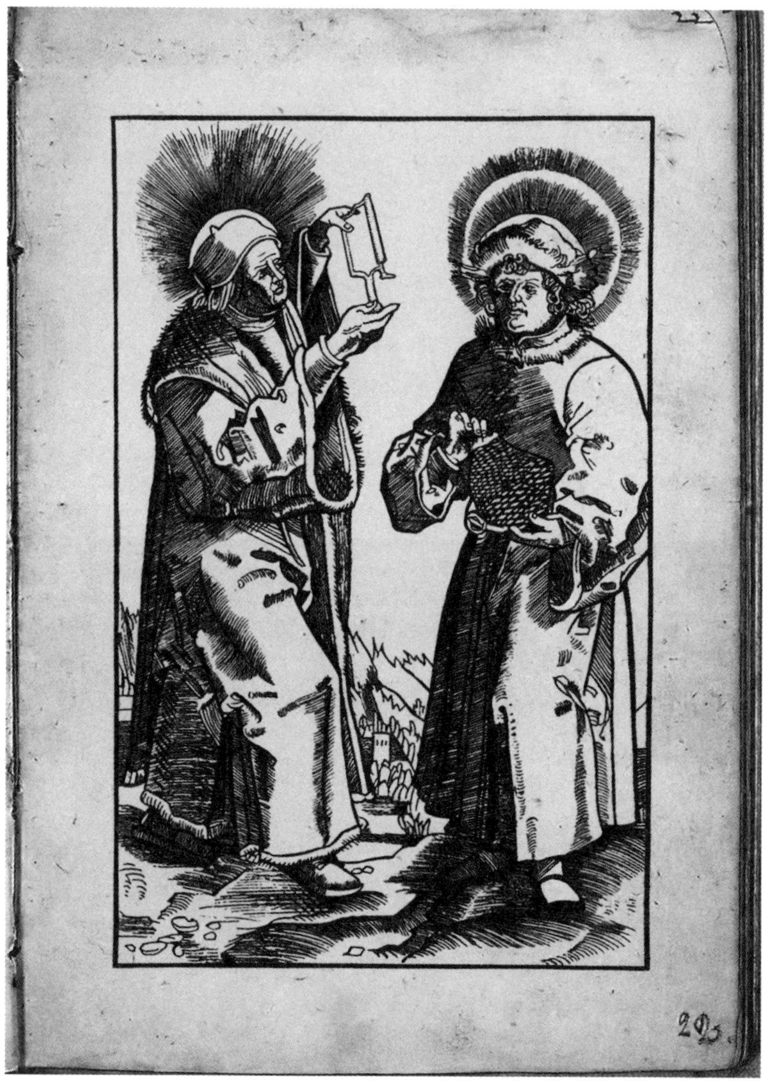

Fig. 4. Woodcut print depicting Saint Mervin Foote,
from the Abbot's Collection, c. 1512.

A replica of the object has been kept in a conservation warehouse in the village of Kent, England, dedicated to preserving medieval artifacts. Despite being mere reproductions, I have decided to include images of detailed replicas of medieval artifacts within this commentary because, even if they challenge the status of the original, these images can elucidate (through their pictorial medium) a passage by which objects can enter into consciousness and the literary imaginary. Such permutation is nestled in the object, which allows the ludic interplay of stimulus and response, an always poetic ensemble. Upon the use or perceptual manipulation of a tool, we encounter an otherness capable of leading us into imaginary voyages that suspend our given immediate reality.

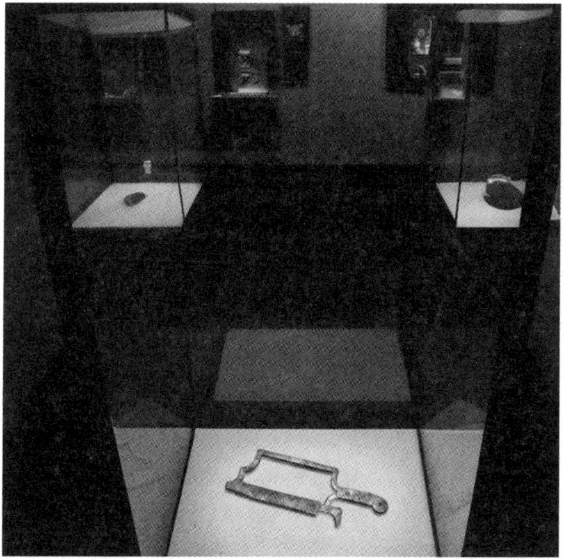

Fig. 5. Museum replica of the object-footer, exhibited in 1998 at the
Kent Medieval Museum, located in rural westeastern England.

As a last deep dive into the symbolical inscription in St. Bede's footer [▭⌐], Stone identifies the highly corporeal and bold connection between the footer and the manicule. Prior to delving into this thought, it is necessary to note that the manicule, from the Latin word *maniculum* meaning "little hand," is a paratextual glyph or sign in the shape of a hand with an extended index finger, typically horizontal (☞). This symbol is commonly used in the margins of manuscripts and printed materials to annotate or draw attention to relevant aspects of the text. In the 12th century, it indicated the beginning of a new paragraph in manuscripts produced in Spain, a practice that continued with the advent of printing. While readers occasionally drew manicules; they were also sometimes provided by scribes or copyists, as in the case of Johannes Gherinx's manuscripts from the year 1462.

Stone draws a parallel between the footnote and the manicule, suggesting that "the history of both, to a great extent, can lend themselves to an anatomical study of textual design, wherein the body appears as a construction reference, and is, in turn, subsumed by the very text it supports and engages with." This parallelism of signs highlights how, from their earliest use in manuscripts, the manicule and the footnote have been a persistent yet changing manifestation of human engagement with textual and cultural artifacts. The manicule and the footnote mark the corporeality of texts and our active encounters with them. Both are metaphorical and utilitarian, ephemeral yet enduring.

The poetics of the foot and the hand have also played essential roles in mnemonics, measurement, mathematical development, and reading patterns, beyond their more familiar appearances in the footer and the manicule.[8] As such, the object-footer and the manicule are inextricably linked to the culture of medieval erudition; the relationship between the physical act of writing and the motor skills of the body was substantially pronounced during this period. This simultaneity of writing and body, text and object, undoubtedly constitutes a crucial lens through which to understand medieval marginalia: an underlying process of embodiment that permeates the surface of every writing, reading, or reader's annotation.

---

[8] Using fingers to recall the 9 times table is a notable example of mnemonics, illustrating the interplay between mathematics and the body. The finger trick works by design, relying on the mathematical properties of the number 9 and the hand structure in the base-10 system.

The body's metaphorical and informative value in design and literature is extensive. Throughout history, images of feet, hands, and fingers have been evoked in religious, mnemonic, cryptographic, and artistic works. For example, in the biblical book of Exodus, we find the finger as a divine metaphor for the act of writing: "And he gave unto Moses when he had made an end of communing with him upon mount Sinai, two tables of testimony, tables of stone, written with the finger of God." The divine hand appears not only in the text of biblical literature but also in later printed pictorial representations and in the Yad pointer used for reading the Torah.

This enduring metaphorical logic extends naturally into the realm of design. Accordingly, we can observe how the body and its extremities are prefigured by objects, which in turn become interpretations of bodily form. The chair exemplifies this relationship: it not only anticipates the presence of a body but also participates in a symbolic game where it interacts at the level of both forms and signs. Having acquired an autonomous form, the convergence of body and language is made evident in metaphorical expressions, such as when referring to the "leg," "arm," "ear," or "foot" of a chair, highlighting the symbiotic entanglement between bodies, language and objects.

In summation, the object-footer remains a case that demonstrates the conjunction of language and body in design, as well as the authorial disorder that arises in the history of the footer.[9] This argument rests on the premise that, just as Stone attributes this phenomenon to the object-footer,

75

---

[9] The footnote, presumably an offspring or tenant of the footer, establishes a certain type of authority stemming from the historian's display of his sources, but also, at the same time, undermines said authority by allowing the reader to trace the same sources and come to conclusions different from those presented. Certain subversive, ambiguous, and destabilizing footnote tropes have been a part of *Approximations to the Object* and of this very commentary. Authors like Jorge Luis Borges, Miguel de Cervantes, Jonathan Swift, Laurence Sterne, Alexander Pope, Jakob Friedrich Lamprecht, and Jean Paul Richter were the first to use footnotes for satirical purposes—whether to ridicule their excessive use in the literature of their time, to invest their narratives with a pretentious academic nature, or to, increase their control over the effects of their narrative by blurring the roles of both author and (fictitious) editor of the work, as in the *Library of Babel* and others. As I append this last footnote, I recognize the way in which my role as author unfolds into that of a reader, making writing and reading simultaneous instances of text. But it is precisely through this unfolding that I am speaking to you. For appended, I am now a reader, and we are in dialogue. I realize how this footnote,

crafted by Mervin Foote and inscribed symbolically by Saint Bede, contemporary authors such as Anthony Grafton and Chuck Zerby have challenged this thesis by attributing the invention of the footnote to other figures. In his celebrated work *The Devil's Details: A History of Footnotes*, Chuck Zerby attributes its invention to the London printer Richard Jugge, who died in 1577.

Perhaps Zerby and Grafton are correct: Bede might not have invented the footer or the footnote. Their attribution rightly proposes the possibility that, just as footnotes appear in such varied forms as to require the most extraordinary ingenuity on the part of the taxonomist, each slight variation must have an organic and unequivocal relationship with the particular historical community in which it was conceived. Even when validating the scholastic practices of medieval monk scribes, heirs of Alexandrian philology, the attribution discounts arguments such as that the use of the footnote and its standardization would only take place several centuries later when the accumulation of historical sources and disputes over their interpretation forced historians to account for their sources methodically. Thus, I have reasoned that the "search for meaning" or "the pursuit of a genesis" is illusory. In the course of this inquiry, I have observed the consistent metonymic displacement of signs as the sole lucid insight in such an endeavor. In this light, the notion of a "meaning fabrication" strikes me as more accurate than that of a "meaning discovery." As Deleuze discusses in *The Logic of Sense*, meaning is never principle or origin, it is something to be produced by new mechanisms.

---

paradoxically, creates a kind of proximity between us: author-reader and reader. I have descended here in order to acquire a new voice. I have left my bedroom in the quiet of Chinatown, New York and have come downstairs to answer the door. I open it here, with my word, at the threshold of this page, the ground floor of the building, to somehow face the questions of my own reader and acknowledge that the production of meaning in literature appears somewhat concealed, unfolding, and incomplete. Most of these footnotes, though you would not expect it, were written almost two years after the main corpus of the commentary was completed. By then, I had become a reader, much as you have, getting lost among the labyrinths and references to Stone, trying to retrieve decisions, lost references, and meanings that could indicate my way out. The reader often forgets that what lies between one page and another—something that, in reading, is inherently invisible as it is made a continuous and immediate activity—may have been, for the author, far from immediate, stretching between each page, hours into years.

Accordingly, just as Stone discloses an object as the predecessor to this phenomenon, there must be various lost accounts, disparate manuscripts, and other corporeal and taxonomic tools that propose alternative mechanisms for structuring text; texts organized in the form of a house (a novel structured as a suburban home for a family of five would have been contrastingly different from one following a spacious mansion owned by a family with an only child); eco-rythmic texts structured according to natural cycles (the sunrise as their beginning and the sunset as their dusk. These writings would have been variable during the different seasons of the year, making winter texts colder and shorter in length); site-specific texts (texts structured for the duration of a specific voyage from a predetermined point A to point B); supermarket texts (a text whose narrator disperses from shelf to shelf, aisle to aisle); mapped texts (Homer's epic poem structured spatially rather than rhapsodically to narrate Odysseus' ten-year journey home. The poem would have been divided into 16 geographical subsections from Troy to Ithaca instead of in its three main thematic sections); cake texts (structured in flavored tiers, with each narrative level building upon the last to create a vertically integrated reading experience. As the reader eats—or reads—each layer introduces a shift in flavor, tone, or texture, culminating in a final symbolic resolution savored with the cherry on top.) See some illustrative examples:

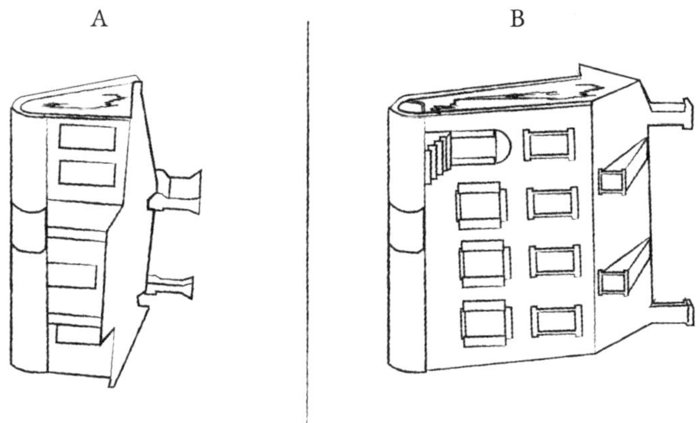

Fig. 6. Novel (a) structured as a suburban home vs.
Novel (b) structured as a spacious mansion.

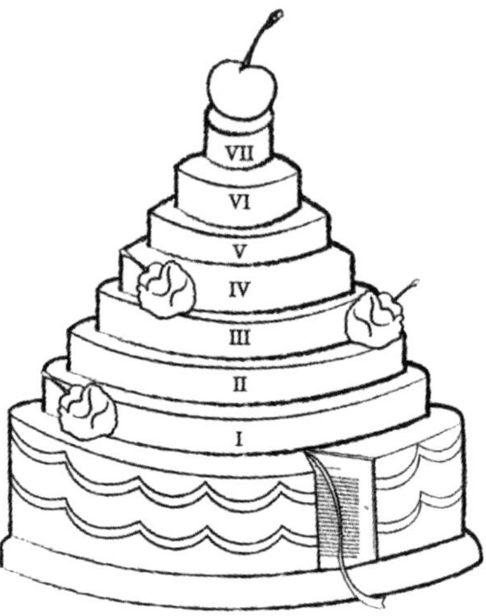

Fig. 7. Cake Texts.

78

Fig. 8. Eco-rythmic Texts.

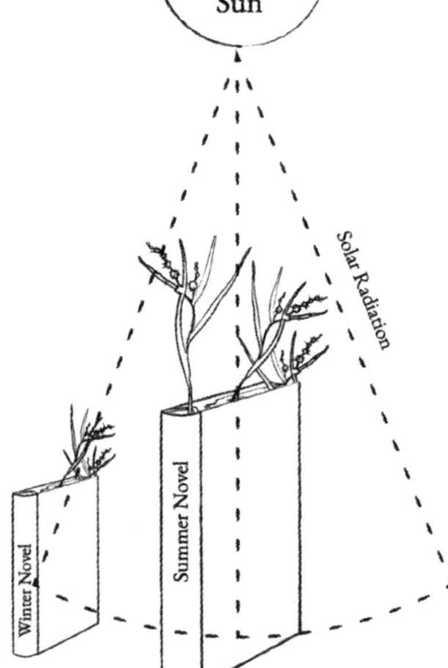

The composition of vast books is a laborious and
impoverishing extravagance. To go on for five hundred
pages developing an idea whose perfect oral exposition is
possible in a few minutes! A better course of procedure
is to pretend that these books already exist, and then to
offer a resume, a commentary... More reasonable, more
inept, more indolent, I have preferred to write notes
upon imaginary books.—Jorge Luis Borges
Prologue to The Garden of Forking Paths

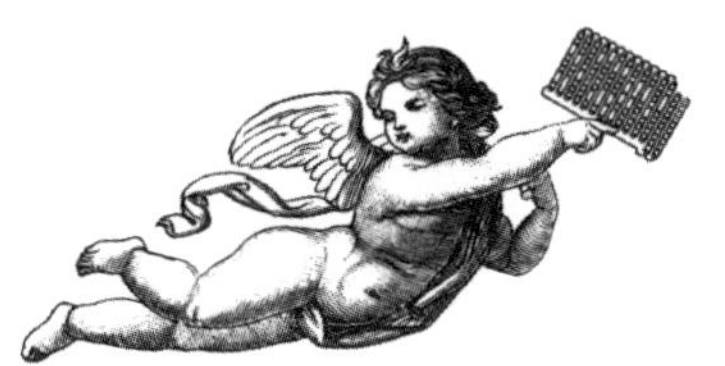

Epilogue (if fictional)
Afterword (if academic)
Truelogue (if made-believed)

I will assign the function of this section to be what a darkroom is for photography. The latter is a small room or cubicle in which all the slits and entrances of light have been covered to prevent any alteration to the chemical substances and material employed in photographic development. Although I will not treat the substance of this text in a chemical manner, this section is destined for the idea of exposure and revelation. Herein, I intend to expose the surgical intervention that design and its objects have exerted upon the narrative, as well as the essential possibilities they have granted as fictional forerunners in the assembly and treatment of the preceding writing.

I deploy scientific words because, just as Victor Frankenstein engineered his creature into existence, I believe that this work has evolved into a chimera whose imaginary vanity threatens the idea of a hegemonic truth, an attack generative of every reader's belief. I have exercised this attack in an alternative manner, one that circumvents violence and instead ascribes itself to an inaudible inquisition, through which I wish neither to destroy nor to upset any being, unlike what the monster would do to William, Elizabeth, and Henry in Mary Shelley's cautionary tale.

> Sorrow only increased with knowledge. Oh, that I had forever remained in my native wood, nor known or felt beyond the sensations of hunger, thirst, and heat! [1]

Henceforth, I invite the readers to enter this room, to the operating theater of fictions and artifices, tricks and contrivances, procedures and surgical instruments: scalpels, tweezers, scissors, specula, tuning forks, hammers, syringes, mouth gags—a space I intend as an emerging discussion, as open-heart surgery.

---

[1] From a special edition of *Mary Shelley's Frankenstein: Annotated for Scientists, Engineers and Creators of all kinds* (p. 99).

Accordingly, the *Commentary on Approximations to the Object* has not only been a personal experiment, a fictional pilgrimage, an academic fiction, a mere excuse, a research study to exercise certain paratextual methodologies through design (which I believe to be possible), but also has expanded into its own question and deafening rhetoric, to which I have, pleasantly, found neither an answer nor a solution. The ambiguity of such an inquiry has been re-incorporated into its very faculty, into its very purpose, and as such, I believe it demands this additional portion, in which I promise to keep a distance from fictional endeavors in order to subject it to a close and proper examination.

This epilogue, which might well be called a *truelogue* or an *aletheia* (the latter being a Greek term often translated as "truth," but more accurately referring to a mode of disclosure or unconcealment, a process of revealing what was previously hidden) is in itself a final climax. And although the plot of this text has not followed Freytag's pyramid in any linear fashion, its climax is rather analogous to the instructions of a magic trick or the patterns of a garment: the exposure of the prosthetic devices needed to sustain any alternative reality, which once revealed, will obliterate all attempts at fantasy, magic, and my credibility as an author, but above all, shall dismantle the vital suspension and immersion techniques necessary for the scaffolding of any world.

In this section, I am terrified to say that the work will acquire for some the deceiving quality of a trick or a bluff and will undoubtedly exist for many between the binary syntax of truth and falsity.[2]

Unfortunately, I feel pressured to affirm that there are rules, limits, and borders to reality (or to what has been demarcated as such), borders that will shape the reader's relationship to the work, and that first drew me towards this writing. Such limits, so stiff and sturdy, are heavily taxing on the imaginary possibilities and ways of being within our exhilaratingly arbitrary world, and are the very ones that have compelled me to comment on, contest, and blur

[2] Fiction, by its nature, involves the creation of imaginary stories, characters, and events. While fiction is not necessarily a "bluff" in the sense of intentionally deceiving or misleading readers, it does involve the art of suspending disbelief and engaging in a willing estrangement of reality.

what exists between the imagined and the real. It is their constraining nature that induces vertigo in me and, consequently, an irrepressible temptation to jump into their impossible cracks. However, recognizing that this work was conceived within such boundaries (given that there is no escape other than to bear them), and specifically that this thesis was bound by an academy that organized it within them, I shall review my work before the attributes of said reality: design problems, authors, citations, image references, among others.

I both admire and mourn whoever chooses to turn a deaf ear and remain ignorant, and fresh, and green; those who will silence this section, or who would be considered by many—but never by me—as "bad readers" for not finishing the book, but who above all will remain with the delirious and detrimental belief of this work as a trustworthy and hermetic entity, and who will humiliate themselves when enthusiastically sharing the cases conceived in this text as veridical findings.

I will also mourn for those who interpret the work purely as a falsehood, a joke, or a provocative trick. My intention has never been to deceive, but rather to distort the conception of reality and the assembly of fiction, manipulating (through design and writing) the structures that incubate meaning.

Despite the unquestionable ironical, apocryphal, and irreverent nature of Stone's work, I feel obliged to clarify that the work is fictional, made-up, invented—or else I am an impostor—when no one has been able to elucidate what "real" really means, particularly in the context of literature.

Hence, I shall admit, as for, as such an omission would undoubtedly allow the work to be labeled as fake, that the majority of the work is indeed fictional, and by the majority, I mean:

i. Stone's treatise titled *Approximations to the Object*
ii. The miscellany in which that treatise was included titled *Meditations on Literary Design*

iii. *Commentary on Approximations to the Object,* a supposed analysis of the aforementioned treatise.

iv. The publisher of *Approximations to the Object,* referred to as *B.P. Corder*

v. *Silas Haslam* and *Herbert Ashe,* other authors published by *B.P. Corder*

vi. The owner of said publisher named *Barret Packington*

vii. The censure of that very publisher by 19th-century English authorities

viii. The friendship and intertextual affinity between Edmund Stone & Samuel Taylor Coleridge

ix. The book written by Coleridge in which this friendship is made evident, titled *Letters, Conversations, and Recollections for an Expanded Literature*

x. The inaugural quote attributed to Michel Foucault in the first section of the commentary

xi. The Greek map and the spatial notion of a mathematical intersection

xii. The *object-sonnet*

xiii. Sonnets I and II alluding to a possible *object-sonnet* as *"the only begetter"*

xiv. The misprinted edition of *The Passionate Pilgrim* binding together Francis Bacon's unfinished tract with the Shakespearean Sonnets

xv. The *Petrarchan object-sonnet*

xvi. The *object-citation* better known as:

xvii. The *Leguminis Citationis,* supposedly acquired by Richard Mead at a Leipzig fair

xviii. A rattle's resemblance to the *fabaceae* family of legumes

xix. *Edward Mervin Foote* and the *object-footer* developed as an amputator

xx. Bede's inscription of that very amputator.

... and the list continues.

In the following paragraphs, I will delve into the inquiries that this work poses, yet try to avoid turning this section into a commentary on the commentary, something I am very propense to do.

An Academic Fiction is Subject to Being Called Fake;
A *Designed Literature* is Subject to Deceive;
Or to Make-Believe too Much

> The fact is that every writer creates his own precursors.
> His work modifies our conception of
> the past, as it modifies the future.
> —Jorge Luis Borges
> *Kafka and his Precursors* in *Other Inquisitions*

> One further remark regarding your many complaints that I
> introduced borrowed expressions into my exposition. I do not deny that
> I did so. It was in fact done deliberately. In the next section of this work,
> if I ever write such a section, I intend to call this topic by its true name
> and to clothe the problem in its historical attire.
> —Guy Debord citing Kierkegaard in *The Society of the Spectacle*

The Michel Foucault quote with which this commentary begins remained intact in its origin, though its concluding lines were subtly manipulated and extended to present, with a certain authentication, the premise that space and knowledge are closely related. Along these lines, the inclusion of an altered quote about the arbitrariness of meaning challenges its own significance through the authority it gains when attributed to a renowned intellectual.

I began to wonder: could Foucault himself refute a quote fictionally positioned within his own discursive framework? Could he, after all, reject such a gesture, having written *What is an Author?* In that same spirit, I questioned, what makes a reader validate an idea simply because it is attributed to a canonical intellectual, or, analogously, a fashion enthusiast validate a garment by virtue of its association with a celebrated brand?[3]

---

[3] How would we read Shakespeare's sonnets if they were not written by Shakespeare? What weight does the author's name carry, and how does attribution shape how we interact with a text? In *What is an Author?* (1969), Michel Foucault reflects on this, noting that: "The disclosure that Shakespeare was not born in the house that tourists now visit would not modify the functioning of the author's name, but, if it were proved that he had not written the sonnets that we attribute to him, this would constitute a significant change (...)" The author's name, like a designer's label seems to operate as a paratextual device that modifies the reception and perception of a piece.

Accordingly, the inclusion of that pseudo-quote marked the beginning of the fictional scaffolding, and at best, a way of suspending all disbelief regarding my "discovery" of the book *Approximations to the Object*.

Misattribution, loose or questionable citations have long been a gesture in the works of other authors, cited within this work, such as Deleuze, Debord, Eco, or Borges. A misattributed phrase in this work therefore functions as an act of subversion and world-building (or world-unbuilding), a trope that seeks to inquire on the logics of authority through which the world and, retroactively fiction, are assembled.[4] As such, to place Foucault's name beneath an altered citation invites the reader to consider the thought *as if* it were his; to see the world through a *Foucauldian* lens. If the phrase resonates, if it bears the weight of his discourse, does it not, in some sense, become his?

After all, Foucault argued that the "author" is a function, not a source. To cite Foucault where he never spoke is not to steal from him, but to assert him; activating the author-function as rhetorical rather than empirical fact. In this view, whoever cites Foucault can cite Stone, and vice versa; as their discourses concern less what is than what could have been under different systems of meaning. This does not equate misattribution in fiction with misinformation, but rather repositions the author as a device through which fiction engages authorship and citation not to guarantee fact, but to simulate the conditions under which a speculative discourse like Stone's might appear.

---

[4] Guy Debord's concept of *détournement* (which has been translated as "displacement") explains how misattribution can serve a substantive purpose: "Détournement is (...) a fragment torn from its own context and development, and ultimately from the general framework of its period and from the particular option (appropriate or erroneous) that it represented within that framework. (...) Its own internal coherence and practical effectiveness are what validate the previous kernels of truth it has brought back into play. Détournement has grounded its cause on nothing but its own truth as present critique." Much like the fictional origin story of the object-citation—a terracotta rattle that becomes ubiquitous across cultures, its origins eroded—the citation similarly complicates notions of truth through its inherent decontextualization. It is precisely this quality that renders truth both unstable and convoluted. Hence, misattribution could be seen as a critical affordance: a reminder that theory is nothing in itself, that it can realize itself only through historical action, and through the historical correction to which it is ultimately bound. Guy Debord, *The Society of the Spectacle*, trans. Ken Knabb (Berkeley: Bureau of Public Secrets, 2014), 110.[1]

No matter the literary precedent for apocryphal tactics, executing this thesis brought my attention to a series of fundamental subjects: the interplay between fabrication and fiction, the shifting dynamics of authorship and authority, and the uneasy distinction between the fake and the fictional. It also underscored the role of authors, the tendency of design projects to resolve rather than to question, the anachronic formats of truth and the function of images. More broadly, it invited reflection-through-play on the fictional possibilities of design, the visuality of fiction, the verges of a text, the construction of intertexts, the transfiguration of meaning, and the strategic use of fictional paratexts.

I believe that the incorporation of design in materializing Stone's made-up treatise infused the work with heightened complexity. Unlike the linguistic or imaginary simulacra found in literature, design offers an immediacy and validity that a text often takes longer to achieve. In this context, design's immediate visuality provokes through appearance, while writing provokes through immersion. What I aim to highlight here is that while fictional design tricks the eye, literary fiction tricks the mind, and, as such, the experience of designing literature implies a far more abrupt, illusory, instantaneous, and intrusive encounter than that of one that is purely textual or designed alone. And precisely because seeing is deeply intertwined with thought—since to see, one must recognize, and to recognize, one must know—the volume, form, and appearance that design offers (and the very fact that the objects of this work exist materially) adds a layer of tangibility to the fictional source. By taking a stance in our immediate material reality, our visual field, they inevitably revise and suspend it.

This suspension invites us to dream, question and imagine. One is left wondering... Does this mean that fiction accrues further validation when instantiated materially? Does the act of materially substantializing fiction reaffirm, or invoke, its existence on another level? Is a *Designed Literature* more real or more fictional? In some way, while the written portion of this fiction enjoys a linguistic existence, its fictional objects go one step further to hold both a

91

linguistic and a material existence in the world. Nonetheless, to only subject the objects from the text to this line of thought would be dismissing the idea that (1) this book is an object, and inversely that (2) the objects within this book are practically printed matter. Differentiating one from the other could be total nonsense! [5]

As such, design emerges as a tool that exposes the way we differentiate what is imaginable from what is conceivable. In this vein, if design is thought of as a discipline that deals with problems and solutions, and if we acknowledge the persistent tension between the useful and the fictional, how might design engage with the challenges posed by literary fiction? If fiction's artifice is not a failure but an ontological condition, how might design problem-solve the frictions between the imaginary and the real? Might we even propose that fiction itself acts as an ambiguous solution (a speculative intervention) that addresses the problems of a narrow reality? These inquiries reveal a dual operation: designing literature entails both generating problems and offering solutions for an imaginary world built *from, of, on, in,* or *about* reality. This invites us to reconsider the Sullivanist axiom of design *form follows function*[6] and ask whether, in some cases, *form follows fiction*[7] or even a *function-fiction*?

Much of the fictional work, such as the personification of Edmund Stone as an academic figure, the design of artifacts and their images, and the positioning of the findings in a credible chronology, consisted of investigating historical sources, but particularly of investigating the ambiguous gaps and holes in their structures. I embarked on the mission to find such cracks and consequently to fill them with imaginary design, to guarantee the reader (or a possible design user) an imperceptible immersion in plausibility.

---

[5] Thoughts on the tension between design and literature in relation to fiction are appended in the errata of this text.

[6] Louis H. Sullivan is often credited with the axiom "form follows function" in the context of architecture and design. This principle emphasizes that the form of an object should be primarily based on its intended function or purpose. See: Louis H. Sullivan, *The Tall Office Building Artistically Considered* (1896).

[7] Bernard Tschumi is credited with coining the axiom "form follows fiction." Tschumi employed this phrase to reference how cultural artifacts, such as literature, can shape and inform architectural design.

When I refer to such holes and gaps, I refer to the historical lacunae, the ambivalence of historical discourse, the parts of stories that remain undocumented, poorly registered or unresolved, whose gaps are neither true nor false, but exist, and, as such, grant permission to be orchestrated by possibilities. Words such as "context" or "frame" facilitated my fabrication of meaning and, more so, constituted my hypothesis of fiction as "fabulation placed in context." To explain the latter, the idea of a hybrid expressed in a speculative formulation has been helpful to me. Let:

a = the contextual or factual embrace of the Shakesperean Sonnets
and Shakespeare's practice,

b = the object-sonnet, an object fabulated from verse,

$\therefore$ when a frames, informs and constricts the emergence of b,

fiction emerges =

$$f(x) = (a+b)$$

93

In this poetic combination, the very essence of fabulation finds its form only when deeply immersed in the rich tapestry of context, allowing fiction to emerge as a hybrid within these dualities: the contextual/factual and the fabulist. One could then go a step further and interrogate more precisely what constitutes A (the contextual/factual), or what exactly defines B (fabulation), in order for F (fiction) to come into being. In doing so, the possibility of fictions existing within fictions exposes reality's endless *mise en abyme*.

The historiographic gaps can thus be conceived as imaginary vessels, spaces that house the fiction, which, in turn, becomes neutralized by its surrounding environment: certain historical facts and designed arti-facts that render the fiction plausible. Nonetheless, upon sharing the early drafts of this work with various colleagues, without an epilogue or a prior disclosure (but surely with a personal note placed on the final page, explaining that the piece had been intended as fiction), the work was, on several occasions, considered "controversial," "deceptive," and/or "fake."

Countless times, I have found myself begging! pleading! asking! for people not to refer to the work as fake. In any case, I assumed that a fiction that both makes use of and is structured around a fictional paratext (which even implied the material development of the elements it enunciates) would, once revealed, inevitably suffer abrupt neutralization due to its resemblance to the aesthetics of truth and its coherent format. After all, the form of the truthful relies on the same rhetorical and visual devices through which truth is signaled, and so it demands a double inversion, and double wit, from the reader to focus less on its content and more on the signs that simulate and perform what is conceived as real. Thus, while a fiction that incorporates the fake may be accused of deception (not because it fails, but precisely because it succeeds in appearing to belong to the real) it should, at last, be taken as an inquiry onto the mechanics of our world.

The distinction between false and fiction becomes a pertinent debate, for this commentary to be set apart from the fake, the latter being something fundamentally different from the former.[8] This tension between truth and fiction and the reasons for making the real and the imaginary collide has been a long-standing debate in the history of ideas, and along these lines, the Argentine author Juan José Saer explains in the *Concept of Fiction* that:

> Fictions are not written to avoid, due to immaturity or irresponsibility, the rigors required by the treatment of the "truth," but precisely to highlight the complex nature of the situation, a complex nature whose treatment is limited to what is verifiable,

---

[8] While the fake actively attempts to be true, the false *is* by default and makes no such attempt *to be* (as it holds a dialectical compromise to truth). Thus "false" no longer simply means "not true." Furthermore a fake imitates reality while the false *is in fact* an error—from, of, and in—reality, and as an error it is a constitutive and temporal part of truth itself. The false gets particularly interesting in the realm of fiction as: what emerges in the fictional use of the false is, thus, not a verifiable/non-verifiable truth, but rather something that is unfit for verification altogether; the false in fiction operates in a space independent of truth-claims. Hence fiction adds another level of ambiguity—while it places one foot in reality, it keeps the other in the realm of the imaginary, never fully claiming the status of the real. In any case, the false can be thought to be, in essence, more "false" than "not true," as the error presupposed for the false *to be* paradoxically grants it a kind of truth-property through its very "not-trueness." This is precisely what Deleuze might refer to as the *Potency of the False*: the false is seen to liberate, through the form of truth, and take on a power of its own.

implying an abusive reduction and impoverishment. By taking a leap towards the unverifiable, fiction infinitely multiplies the possibilities of a treatment. It does not turn its back on a supposed objective reality; quite the contrary, it immerses itself in its turbulence, disdaining the naive attitude that consists of pretending to know in advance how that reality is made. It is not a surrender to the ethics of truth but the search for a slightly less rudimentary one.

Fiction is not, therefore, a vindication of the false. Even those fictions that incorporate the false in a deliberate way—false sources, false attributions, confusion of historical data with imaginary data, etc—do so not to confuse the reader but to point out the double character of fiction, which inevitably mixes the empirical and the imaginary. This mix, displayed only in certain types of fiction until it becomes a constitutive aspect of its organization, as could be the case of some Borges stories or Thomas Bernhard novels, is nevertheless present to a greater or lesser extent in all fiction, from Homer to Beckett. The paradox of fiction is that if it resorts to the false, it does so to increase its credibility. The muddy mass of the empirical and the imaginary, which others have the illusion of dividing at their own will into the slices of truth and falsehood, leaves the author of fiction with only one possibility: to immerse himself in those.

But fiction does not ask to be believed as truth, but as fiction. Such desire is not an artist's whim but the first condition of its existence because only by being accepted as such will it be understood that fiction is not the fictionalized exposition of a certain ideology but a specific treatment of the world, inseparable from its thematic. This is the essential point of the whole problem, and it must always be kept in mind to avoid confusion of genres. Fiction keeps its distance both from the prophets of the truth and from the euphorics of the false. (Saer, Juan José. *El Concepto de Ficción*, 2014, p.11)

By the same token, Stanley Cavell, in *The Seen World: Reflections on the Ontology of Cinema*, comments: "It is a poor idea of fantasy which takes it to be a world apart from reality, a world clearly showing its unreality. Fantasy is precisely what reality can be confused with. It is through fantasy that our conviction of the worth of reality is established; to forgo our fantasies would be to forgo our touch with the world" (Cambridge, MA: Harvard University Press, 1979, p.85).

It seems that fiction, then, operates within an undeniable paradox: even when resorting to the unverifiable and incorporating falsehoods (unlikely to be legitimized), it does so under its own logic to broaden the vantage point and expand the range of engagement with the world. Verisimilitude thus becomes an essential resource, not to reinforce the probable or actual state of affairs, but to open imaginative pathways towards alternative realities.

As a pivot to contemporary design discourse, designers Anthony Dunne and Fiona Raby debate the perplexity of the "real" in *Design for the Unreal World in Studio Time, Future Thinking in Art and Design*:

> The phrase "real world" is something most designers (and academics) will be familiar with—as a rallying cry, as a critique, as a justification. But what is this real world, and where is it? More importantly, this suggests there is also a "not real world:" where does this not exist? And who decides what is real and what is not (what can and what can not exist)? Speaking as committed objectologists fascinated by objects of all kinds whether real or unreal, we both find it perplexing, when confronted with a certain kind of object, to hear a person claim that it is not real. Yet, there in front of us is a thing, taking up space, existing, being in the world. Ok, the values it embodies might be at odds with those around us, and its purpose or reason for existing might be abstract or cerebral, but surely, if it actually exists as a physical object, it is real.

This binary view, which divides the world of ideas, things, and thoughts into "real" and "not real," is extremely damaging to the fostering of imagination and its ability to uncover alternatives to how things are now. Especially when the word "unrealistic" often simply means "undesirable" to those in charge, rendering alternative realities impossible for everyone else. Designers need to move beyond this binary approach to dividing up thoughts, ideas and things. They all exist after all, just in different ways, somewhere, otherwise it would not even be possible to think of them. Design needs more nuanced ways of understanding and talking about this relationship, one that acknowledges that the real and the not real are just two poles on a subtle and rich spectrum. (Dunne & Raby, from an entry shared in www.designedrealities.org).

Dunne & Raby's critique of the rigid binary between the "real" and "not real" in design aligns with Alexius Meinong's *Theory of Objects,*[9] a philosophical inquiry into the nature of existence. This theory serves to explain that (1) there are objects that do not exist and (2) every object that does not exist is yet constituted in some way and thus may be the subject of true predication. Distinguishing between an object's *Sosein* (character) and *Sein* (existence), Meinong argues that every object has the characteristics it has independently of whether it exists. In short, his example of a round square exemplifies that non-existent objects can possess properties that make them the target of thought. Traditional metaphysics, he claims, has a "prejudice in favor of the real," overlooking the broader range of thinkable objects. Hence, Meinong's theory opens the door to considering fictional, hypothetical, or contradictory entities as ontologically relevant, despite their lack of actual being.

In this manner, *Approximations to the Object* engages in a *phenomenontological,* designed and epistemic game, allowed by language's dual capacity to gen-

---

[9] Dunne & Raby's video *Meinong's Jungle (Theory of Objects)* uses Alexius Meinong's *Theory of Objects* as a framework to expand the aesthetic and conceptual boundaries of design. Such inquiry visualizes the theory and could be regarded as an exercise on designing existence.

erate and distort meaning (its semantic operations that render reality think-able, yet also refract and convolute it), the gaps of history, and the materialities of fictional objects. If *phenomenontology* emerges from philosophical fiction it is as, for to comment on Stone's treatise, one must first come up with a metaphysics of *Designed Literature*, in order to then address the metaphysics of its existence (i.e. what his artifacts are or how they come into appeerance).

Objects herein emerge from an active engagement between conception, narration, materialization and imagination. Like language, design becomes not only a response to functional needs, but a material agency that shapes reality —making imagination and fiction a generative material process as well, capable of bypassing the usual indeterminacy of fictional objects, the presumed determinacy of real ones, as well as the language we use to explain them.[10]

The objects presented in Stone's treatise thus expose a potentiality in material conceptual constructs, as these emerge within the designerly and literary, and yet remain contradictory; they are neither entirely material nor entirely conceptual. Such *phenomenontological* exercise takes place as the objects depicted in the story have been crafted to become a constitutive part of its paratext and simultaneously claim their place in the physical realm.

---

[10] It is useful to consider Wittgenstein's concept of language-games (*Sprachspiele*), where meaning emerges from the way in which language is used within a specific context rather than through a fixed reference to reality. Kendall Walton builds on this with his theory of make-believe, emphasizing the role of pretense in both the creation and reception of fiction. According to Walton, fictional discourse operates within a language-game distinct from that of non-fictional reference; and yet, it is within the latter that we seek real theories for various kinds of fictional objects. Consequently, the search for a real ontological status of fictional objects thrives in complexity, as it misapprehends the incommensurability between these distinct games; attempting to translate meaning across fundamentally incompatible modes of reference. Still, while fiction and non-fiction operate in separate registers, the latter undeniably conditions the former, allowing for a generative treatment through which fiction evolves into its own world-logic. Paradoxically, in that very process, the constructed fictional world often excludes its own creator. Thus, stipulating a (doomed) fictional ontology confined to the particular fictional language-game should be considered instead, rather than attempting to bridge the unbridgeable gap between fictionality and reality. In this spirit, design emerges as an effective device to bypass ontological deadlocks by creating objects that exist between categories. Ultimately, it is the materiality introduced by design that inaugurates and actualizes a whole new kind of fictional game—unsolvable by language, yet concrete enough to build (through matter) a bridge between the imaginary and the real.

The artifice is real. The object-sonnet is a real wooden toy. The object citation is a real clay rattle. The object-footer is a real steel amputator. Hence, their possibilities to be experienceable through sensorial contemplation and enter, appear in the space of imagination and consciousness, expose the contradictions of what we call "real," or alternatively, ratifies the power of fiction, all of which—no matter the distinction—are experienced in "reality," in experience, in the now, and as such, morph into thought and consciousness. Fiction can never be absent from its being!

Yet, even if these real artifices are shaped by human design and narrative, their existence and experiencability should not be solely reduced to human awareness, despite the fact that their significance, function, and form emerge from a confluence of both material conditions and human intentions. In this sense, even though the adoption of an ontological commitment with merely possible objects may not exert a total effect across all strata of reality, fictions that are concretized and designed can nonetheless give rise to new modes of existence, or inquiries on such; metaphysical meditations conditioned by the actualizations of fictional worlds. In doing so, possible worlds are made to exist in the actual world, transmuting possibilia into realia.[11]

---

[11] The *Possibilist Theory* would argue that fictional entities do not exist in our actual world but instead exist in possible worlds; alternative realities where the events of fiction are true. In this sense, fictional entities are similar to other "merely possible" beings, such as talking donkeys. According to the SEP entry on *Possible Worlds*, some things that do not exist in our world, like talking donkeys, can exist in these other possible worlds. As such, the *Possibilist Theory* would claim that a character like *Edmund Stone* from *Commentary on Approximations to the Object* does not exist in our world, but rather exists in some possible world where the treatise *Approximations to the Object* is a real, historical work. However, retreating to the possibilist view that *Edmund Stone* has such properties only in merely possible worlds carries its own costs; for it seems to underestimate the role of the actual world in devising this fictional character and would diminish the actual, material existence of the objects he studies, mutually subordinating them solely to that possible world. This work, however nuanced, demonstrates that while fictional characters like *Edmund Stone* can only ever be posited within fictional discourse (as *intentional objects* or non-actual entities that come about through narrative, imagery, or description) and remain confined by the *Possibilist Theory*, the fictional objects he studies can achieve a different kind of existence through their physical manifestation. While not identical to their fictional counterparts, these physical instantiations (replicas of a fiction) establish a unique bridge between possible and actual worlds that evolves mere subsistence as, materially speaking, they come to exist. They are not reproductions of fictional objects so much as transformations of fiction into a new kind of entity. Unlike Stone himself, who shall be confined to the realm of fiction, his objects can cross the boundary into a material reality: becoming new kinds of entities altogether—not purely fictional (since they exist physically) and perhaps not purely actual either (since their origin and meaning derive from a fictional premise).

There is thus an ontology to this fiction, in its eagerness to assemble worlds that contest the reality that hosts it, and a fictional ontology to that ontology as well. As Karen Barad argues in *Meeting the Universe Halfway*, knowing does not simply imply representing an external reality, but rather enacts a material and discursive process that constructs reality as it unfolds. They state that "we are responsible for the world of which we are a part, not because it is an arbitrary construction of our choosing, but because reality is sedimented out of particular practices that we have a role in shaping and through which we are shaped." (Barad, *Meeting the Universe Halfway*, p. 390)

Consequently, if this work is understood as a design experiment, a material-discursive apparatus that realizes a particular configuration of the world, a creature that, once released, is absolved and becomes autonomous—then the very discursive and material practices enacted in its fiction participate in an epistemic, performative, joint construction of reality.

100   *Designed literatures* can thus serve both as physical and linguistic formulations of a world, inquiring into the materiality and language of meaning-making as conditions for possibility. Even while the fictional hypothesis presented herein is fallible, error-tolerant, and not fully bound by classical logic or empiricism, as this commentary manipulates, it emerges and collapses; it exposes congruence and inconsistency; it strives and fails; it gathers and offers revelations. As it manipulates, it renders and fractures the intelligible, and what remains is a paralogic exercise in the intimate relationship between materialities and concepts, i.e., design and literature, matter and language, objects and texts.

Readers who enter this game of fluxes are left with no choice but to believe in the reality of the tools authors employ to manipulate, build and write their worlds, eventually leading them to entrust the objects (no less than the tools) with that same confidence.

> *For, what is it of this pen that allows me to pen this?*
> *For, what is it of this word that allows me to word this?*
> *For, what is it of this essay that allows me to essay this?*

Object-Telling and Story-Making in
Approximations to the Object

> The genealogist needs history to dispel the chimeras of the
> origin, somewhat in the manner of the pious philosopher
> who needs a doctor to exorcize the shadow of his soul.
> —Michel Foucault, *Nietzsche, Genealogy, History*

The fabrication of origin, materialized in Stone's designed objects as precursors of meaning, functions not only to establish narrative authority, but also to critique the solemnity bestowed upon it. In this context, origin is not treated as an unquestionable point of beginning, but rather as a rhetorical and aesthetic device that exposes its own artifice. It is nothing more than a "metaphysical extension that arises from the belief that things are more precious and essential at the moment of birth," states Foucault in *Nietzsche, Genealogy, History*. Thus, endowing design objects (or any cultural creation) with a fabricated origin allowed Stone's character to acquire a kind of transcendental legitimacy, simply by accessing the "originals" and gaining symbolic authority from them. (This move also brings to the surface the tension between the original and the reproduced, as one could suppose that an original presumes a copy.)[12]

However, the notion of origin as something inherently precious, lofty, or essential dissolves into a metaphysical illusion, an unfounded belief, once one realizes it is a construct shaped by intervention, interpretation, narration, replication, and transformation. Foucault's claim underscores that nothing is intrinsically true at the beginning: there is nothing to unveil.

---

[12] Upon materially transforming the *possibilia* of *Approximations to the Object* into *actual* and *concrete possibilia* (by means of materially fabricating the objects that the text comments on) the reader faces the challenge on what there is and about what kinds of things reality includes. Much as with the object-sonnet, the object-citation and the object-footer, one encounters an ever-diminishing and contradictory literature on the existence of such types of objects. In order to not overcomplicate their existence, I hereby agree to destroy the replicas under my possession if the original exemplars of such invented artifacts are to be found.

Rather, the significance of origin arises from an artificial elevation that grants the original an almost spiritual status, when in reality, it is shaped not by purity but by singularities, accidents, deviations, errors, misinterpretations, and the forces that give it a definite form and name. The paradox, then, is that authenticity does not reside in some pure, mythical, untouched beginning but rather in the contaminated narratives and constructs we generate; so long as we recognize their artificiality.

By the same token, the artificial meaning of this work was assembled in the manner of a chimera, whose incoherent form fades away to remain in the word, to signify the imaginary or illusory, an idea or concept that seems to be real but is not. "False idea," and "vain imagination" is the definition of chimera now found in many dictionaries. Before that, the chimera in Greek mythology was a female monster with a lion's head, goat's body, and serpent's tail. Seen this way, the figure becomes a metaphor for the imaginary and fantastic nature of writing. A story once told to me by an Argentine rabbi illustrates this well. In it, a Jewish scribe, upon realizing that design and language could both mirror and generate reality, set out to compose a *midrash* containing all conceivable elements: from an alternative Hebrew alphabet to speculative reliquaries. His oeuvre, much like Borges' tales, offered an account of an alternative Judaic imaginary, inscribed, purposefully, on the skin of a chimera.

This creature is thus illustrative of literature's and design's capacity to conjure an otherworld through languages and materials that blend both the real and the unreal; worlds, beings and objects that once lived only in the mind and that, even if they do not ascribe to reality, are nevertheless captured on matter.

It is precisely this, both the chimera's illusory quality and its assemblage (a creature formed by parts with different origins), makes it instrumental in describing the writing procedure of *Commentary on Approximations to the Object*, which corresponds to a style that is, to me, *Designed Literature*.[13]

---

[13] In conversation with the publisher of the book, Freek Lomme, categorizing the work was delightfully appealing for its contradiction. Hence, the attempt to classify *Commentary on Approximations to the Object* was particularly challenging as, besides the already existing book categories (such as novels,

It was the objects that I devised before my writing (in the first instance only visualized as sketches and renders) that appeared as ambiguous imaginary vessels, *chimerized* between an array of literary terms (such as the format of a sonnet, the symbol of a quotation and the structure of a footer) and design procedures such as prototyping and graphic imaging. Such hybrids presented themselves as fictional objects, which I named after their literary origins, and which became devices to craft and tell a story. In the realm of the writing, they were not only the pretext by which I engaged in "object-telling" but also the fictional paratextual tools incorporated into the commentary's fictional scaffolding.

The aforementioned hybrids eventually found their material texture by evolving their fictional images into tangible objects. This permutation blurs the line between fiction and reality, the imaginable and the existing. Such combinations of apparently incompatible elements prove that the creation of literary worlds is also possible from design and that designed artifacts hold the potential to function both as fictional triggers and as literary devices reincorporated into a text: suppose a writer is to contemplate and write from experience, what, then, does it mean to fabricate something fictional, to experience its fictional *thingness*, and turn back to the blank page to write a narrative capable of framing it and justifying it (as an object of design)?

In this way, design has served me as a fictional resource, a tool for imagining, a device to instrumentalize the paratext, and, in turn, use the latter as an apparatus to make-believe. Coincidentally, the words *imagining* and *imaging* resonate semantically; thus, if we ponder imagination as the capacity to produce images, and imaging as a constitutive exercise of imagining, design proposes a vast array of methodologies to do so.

---

essays, treatises, etc), there is yet to exist a more unsettling and sparse order to organize these kinds of works: that of books that exist without existing, of texts that subsist without being, of objects that are texts and texts that are objects, and so on. Acknowledging the arbitrariness of every classification system, and intending to resist most established categorizations, the term *Designed Literature* was selected. Other terms discussed in the process were: *Fictional Non-Fiction, 'Pataphysics, Speculative Non-Fiction, Academic Fiction, Paratextual Fiction, Philosophical Fiction, Experimental Literature, Parafiction, Pseudobiblia, Paracademic Literature, Among Others.*

In an attempt of order, with which I do not intend to impose a logical explanation on a highly rhizomatic and multi-step process like that of making/writing this thesis, the project initially consisted of readings. Those readings then derived into translating specific literary terms into objects (formats to forms), initially displayed as renders, images that allowed the text to develop as a periphery; making the writing in this work a suburb. Through this multi-layered research-through-making approach, the pictures of the objects began raising ideas such as "object-telling," "story-making," and "maybe-objects," but essentially, the question: How can these fictional objects assume a literary function through the unfolding of a writing that both justifies their existence and re-incorporates them (as fictional devices) into its paratext—treating them as ambivalent, illusory exercises in verisimilitude, as well as characters essential to the development of a plot?

After deploying writing as a peripheral framing of the object I decided to reproduce them materially. I intentionally use the word "reproduce" (to produce again) since these objects had already existed as fictional entities prior to their materialization. It was only later that, through the robust presence they took on the physical world, they became altogether fictional, concrete, actual, and abstract objects. Such an exercise existed between the margins of design and literature—parafictionally[14] bleeding into reality from the imaginary, pushing the ontology of fiction from designed appearances. It was through this relay between narrative and design that my inquiry reflected on the design mechanisms through which fiction renders itself plausible.

---

[14] "Parafictionally" is an invented adjective I have derived from the term "parafiction," coined by art historian Carrie Lambert-Beatty. In her essay *Make-Believe: Parafiction and Plausibility,* she uses this term to describe an emergent genre of artwork that exists in the overlap between fact and fiction: "Like a paramedic as opposed to a medical doctor, a parafiction is related to but not quite a member of the category of fiction as established in literature and drama. It remains a bit outside. It does not perform its procedures in the hygienic clinics of literature, but has one foot in the field of the real." Thus, it is the parafictional nature of Edmund Stone and his objects, both visual and material, positioned between the imaginary and the real, that could lead to the framing of the paraobject or the paraphilosopher in fiction. These entities, whose origins stem from the real, selectively employ facts that are useful, and carefully disregard those that might contradict them, constructing a "real" whose narrative is not just textual but designed, partial, artificial, unstable, and convoluted. Such tropes assert the veracity of the made-up (parareality) through the lens of what has already been validated as real—and unreal—thereby challenging the very foundations of the site from which the audience or reader typically engages.

Certain "formats of truth," such as an object placed before us on a table, serif typefaces typically associated with academic authority, an archival image, a quote, a map, or a reference to a posthumous author, resemble one another in their capacity for producing certain interventions that render them credible, given a certain context, even if their substance is fictional. Accordingly their way of being presented offers them a provisional legitimacy, essential for hijacking its original function and operating as speculative *asifs;* Trojan Horses capable of infiltrating the nature of reality. And, while fiction need not be believable to be thinkable, design's visual and material cues heavily rely on the real to build on the imaginary, thereby producing a verisimilitude that negotiates between perceived belief and constructed illusion.

This is not to say that the point of *designed literatures* is to misinform, nor to aestheticize deception; rather, they engage in a suspension of disbelief that allows fiction to emerge as an intellectual pleasure; a speculative mode of worlding enriched by the designer's engagement with the rules of reality (perspective, texture, light, shadow, scale, typography, gravity, color, etc.) only to subvert and revise its own constructedness.

It is, therefore, both a challenge and an opportunity to write and make fiction with the tools of design, precisely because such tools draw from, and risk overextending, the logic of the physical world. Yet, it is this very capacity that dramatizes the instability of meaning and is rigorous for highlighting the fictionality of fiction, as even when it maneuvers the conditions through which the world is constructed, it exposes its mechanics, its scams, its loopholes; suggesting that reality (in a manner not unlike) is an effort rather than a given.

The interplay between appearance and suspension of disbelief became a central exploration in this research, particularly regarding the role design might play in the paratext of literary fiction. I wondered: How can an image, a design, an object—an appearance—manifest in a written fiction to push (through its paratextual entity) the margins of the text?[15]

---

[15] It is interesting to consider the term "bleed" in graphic design, which refers to visual elements extending beyond the page's edge. Metaphorically, a design bleed could also suggest the spill of imagination into reality.

Gérard Genette, a French literary theorist and linguistic scholar known for his foundational contributions to narratology and structuralist literary criticism, emerged as an indispensable figure at the final stages of this research. Although he does not specifically elaborate on the use of designed fictional paratexts (a practice I encountered for the first time in Borges' fictional footnotes and editor's notes), Genette provides a clear and expansive definition of paratextuality. The critic maintains that:

> The literary work consists, exhaustively or essentially, of a text, that is, a more or less long sequence of verbal statements that contain more or less meaning. But that text rarely appears in its naked state without the reinforcement and accompaniment of a certain amount of verbal productions, such as the author's name, title, preface, and illustrations. It is not always known whether they should be considered belonging to the text or not, but in any case, they surround and extend it, precisely to present it in the usual sense of this verb, but also in its strongest sense: to make it present, to ensure its presence in the world, its "reception" and consumption, in the form, at least nowadays, of a book. The accompaniment, of variable size and style, constitutes what he has called elsewhere, in accordance with the frequently ambiguous meaning of this prefix in French—adjectives like *parafiscal* or *paramilitary*—the paratext of the work. Thus, the paratext is, for us, the means by which a text becomes a book and proposes itself as such to its readers and, more generally, to the public. Instead of a sealed-border or limit, in this case, we are dealing with a threshold, or—as Borges used it in regards to the preface—with a "vestibule" that offers anyone the possibility to enter or turn back: "an undecided zone" between the interior and exterior, without rigid limits, whether towards the interior (the text) or towards the exterior (the world's discourse about the text), a border, or as Philip Lejeune said, "the edge of the printed text that, in reality, controls all reading." This fringe, indeed, always carrying authorial com-

ments more or less legitimized by the author, constitutes, between the text and what is outside it, a zone not only of transition but of transaction; the privileged site of a pragmatics and a strategy. (Gérard Genette and Marie Maclean, "Introduction to the Paratext," New Literary History 22, no. 2 (1991): 261).

Considering the compelling event in which the paratext was the pretext of the text and was later reincorporated as a fictional device, I reflect on this work as the *deviceing* of a written story: a theory and practice-based process that instrumentalizes design both as a narrative trope and as the physical means for staging fiction through constructed form.

Herein, design was folded two-dimensionally into a book. Set design and prop design in theatre or film serve as analogies for how design was implemented in this writing, which paradoxically results in a literature that is a dramaturgy of the object, a literary design, a designed literature, a paratextual fiction. Objects herein have been *deviced* to become the objects of a fictional spectacle.

Rather than only depicting the fictional world of the commentary, these designed objects punctuate how reality is constructed, seen and understood. They play with our assumptions and rely on our perceptual relationship to the world around us. As German philosopher Markus Gabriel discusses in *Fictions*, the nature of reality and our relationship to it is not something we can easily escape: "Appearance is being. We do not escape from reality by deceiving ourselves or by being deceived about it. The real is that from which we cannot distance ourselves. Every attempt to escape fails, because we are involved, because what we are trying to escape from (reality) is modified at most through our imagination. No thought or activity makes it disappear. The spirit of the times is the current constellation in each case of an appearance that legitimizes certain fallacies in congruences, which dissipate when considered more carefully philosophically."

In consonance with the last point, the visuality that design grants, embodied in the two-dimensional images found within the text and in the three-dimensional objects reproduced, is, exists, at least in its appearance. And even if these designs exist and are strengthened within a fictional structure, they effectively bring us closer to the unrelenting manner in which reality is intimated and becomes perpetually established—a reality we neither fully recognize nor can distance ourselves from.

Paradoxically, when the simulacrum of appearances is revealed, it highlights the narrow margin by which we validate said reality, precisely by confronting us with our rare ability to critically distance ourselves from it; becoming at once the dreamer and the *dremee*, subjects both shaping and being shaped. The employment of verisimilitude in visual languages developed for fiction's sake thus scrutinizes how we relate to, recognize, and certify the given world, and thereby, fiction.

108   Once we wake from the commentary in which we dream—or are dreamt by, —Stone, the objects of his study remain materialized before us. A fantasy by Coleridge comes to mind: someone dreams they cross through paradise and are given a flower as proof. Upon waking, the flower remains. What, then, are these type of objects? In much the same way, Stone's designed artifacts suture the conceptual wound between the material and the fictional. These thought-objects prevail as the metaphysical residue of an illusion. Their inversions suggest a provocative question: if the objects of a fiction can be real, then might their readers, or spectators, be fictional?

Therefore, the status of this work, as a being in-between, of amphibious nature, suspended between belief and disbelief, truth and falsehood, fact and speculation, proposes its location within the wide fictional heterocosm, among a range of other non-real, fictional or quasi-real ontologies. In this way as the writing of *Commentary on Approximations to the Object* is composed of a definitive combination of the twenty-odd orthographic symbols of the alphabet, such is to reside on one of the twenty shelves within one of the infinite hexagonal galleries in Borges's *Library of Babel*. Or, more precisely, on a shelf within the *Crimson Hexagon*.[16]

This fiction exists within the prior. This fiction is **HYPERFICTION.**

I now long to stumble upon an analogous site where I can preserve the physical objects bifurcated from the text (an object's material resistance is unlike the portability of language). Such longing is proof of the futility of my endeavor; a failure in attempting to fold such artifacts within this very page.

109

---

[16] In *The Library of Babel*, a short story by Jorge Luis Borges, the narrator conceives the universe as a vast, infinite library filled with books containing every possible combination of the twenty-two orthographic symbols. Most of these books are meaningless gibberish, but somewhere within the library exist books that contain all knowledge, truth, and every possible work of literature. The *Crimson Hexagon* appears as a brief and mysterious section of the library containing books that are "smaller than usual, all-powerful, illustrated, and magical." The *Crimson Hexagon* thus presents a contradiction, a heterotopia (or a space for deterritorialization) within the rigid and all-encompassing structure of the library. While every other book in the library follows the same character set and size, lacks illustrations, and possesses no supernatural qualities, the *Crimson Hexagon* appears to defy them all.

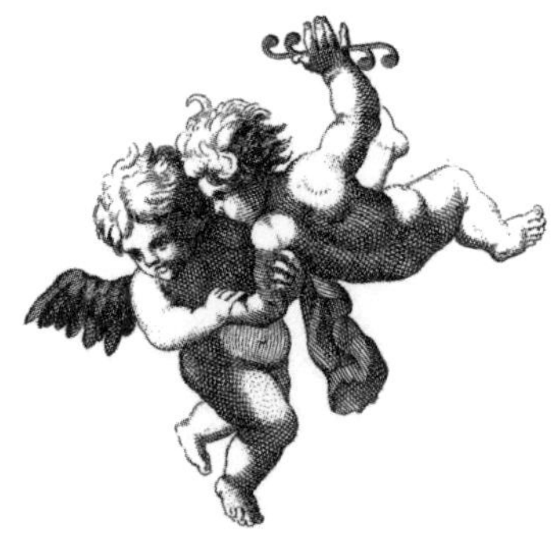

ERRATA

Page 5: the misprinted empty footnote should read: Edmund Stone (1770–1812), author of *Approximations to the Object,* is often confused with Edmund Stone FRS (c. 1690 – March or April 1768), an autodidact Scottish mathematician who lived in London and primarily worked as an editor of mathematical and scientific texts. The confusion between these two figures is understandable, as the dates and places of birth for both remain proximus yet obscure, as do the names of their parents. This ambiguity has yet to be resolved in academic circles due to a lack of sufficient documentation.

Page 5: *Letters, Conversations, and Recollections for an Expanded Literature* is officially titled *Poetical Works of Coleridge and Keats, Volume 1.*

Page 13: The altered Michel Foucault quote "In any given culture and at any given moment, the mutations between objects and language have proved to be interchangeable, yet too exposed to the vagaries of chance or imagery for it to be supposed that their history could be anything other than irregular. It was, in fact, the human attempt to make sense of that primary, incomprehensible, and once uninhabited space that led to the arbitrary archaeology of knowledge in Western thought." should instead read: "The other disciplines, however those, for example, that concern living beings, languages, or economic facts are considered too tinged with empirical thought, too exposed to the vagaries of chance or imagery, to age-old traditions and external events, for it to be supposed that their history could be anything other than irregular. At most, they are expected to provide evidence of a state of mind, an intellectual fashion, a mixture of archaism and bold conjecture, of intuition and blindness. But what if empirical knowledge, at a given time and in a given culture, did possess a well-defined regularity? If the very possibility of recording facts, of allowing oneself to be convinced by them, of distorting them in traditions or of making purely speculative use of them, if even this was not at the mercy of chance? If errors (and truths), the practice of old beliefs, including not only genuine discoveries, but also the most naive notions, obeyed, at a given moment, the laws of a certain code of knowledge?" Michel Foucault, *The Order of Things: An Archaeology of the Human Sciences* (New York: Vintage Books, 1994, p.14).

Page 17: *Approximations to the Object,* Introduction: "We have been misled into thinking that objects emerge only and exclusively subsequent to the story, rather than to think that the story and its formats have ever succeeded the objects." should instead read: "We have long been led astray by the erroneous supposition that objects arise solely and necessarily in the wake of the tale, as though the narrative were their rightful antecedent. Yet, upon due reflection, it is far more reasonable to discern that the tale, with all its forms and modes, has ever been the successor to the objects themselves." Edmund Stone, *Approximations to the Object: A Tentative Towards a Literature of Things* (Northumberland: B.P Corder, 1827, p.2).

Page 90: The footnote on Guy Debord designates another sub-footnote that should read: Borges's story of *Pierre Menard, Author of the Quixote* complicates the concepts of attribution—and thus misattribution—*détournement*, and even plagiarism. Menard, an eccentric 20th-century French writer, polymath, and former reader of Cervantes, composes a manuscript that is identical to Miguel de Cervantes's *Don Quixote.* Yet, rather than replicating, translating, or rewriting the novel, Menard independently produces it word by word, thereby presenting a paradox in authorship: a work can be verbally the same and yet ontologically distinct. Literary works, Borges suggests, do not exist merely as static texts but come alive through the reader's active engagement. Each reader writes their own *Quixote*, amending the text, enriching it with shifting interpretations, and imbuing it with different consequences across time. When Menard writes "the truth, whose mother is history," he constructs a radically different philosophical proposition than what Cervantes had done with those exact words, even while the text remains the same, the act of reading it under Menard transforms its significance through new historical and philosophical contexts. The story thus proposes a paralogism of attribution, demonstrating how context and authorship fundamentally alter meaning, and that identical texts may become genuinely different works. This paradox suggests that misattribution need not be understood merely as deception, but rather as subversion; while it maintains a relationship with the original text and author, it moves beyond it, altering it in order to emancipate it. Moreover, it reveals how each reader (who, in Borges's game is interchangeable with the writer) ultimately writes their own version of a text, affording to do so on different levels of engagement, regardless of whether the text exists in a material sense or not; meaning transcends mere textual identity and emerges in the dynamic interplay between creator and receptor.

Page 92: The full extent of the discussion between design and literature's ontology and phenomenology should read:

This gives rise to an intriguing tension between design and literature in relation to fiction, as both disciplines give rise to fictional entities through different modalities: literature does so through semantic and narrative construction, while design instantiates form through visual and material means. However, in the case of *Commentary on Approximations to the Object*, these fields intertwine, producing fictional entities that are simultaneously textual and material, conceptual and physical. This convergence demands a reconsideration of the categories through which we understand fictional existence.

Literary works often contain open-ended spaces (zones of semantic or imaginative indeterminacy) that are activated by the reader's interpretation. In this sense, the act of reading partially fleshes out the skeletal framework laid by the author, rendering it more "concrete" in the reader's mind. Yet, when design introduces a pictorial and/or material dimension into literature, it extends the traditional understanding of concretization beyond the mental. Such is the case of this *Commentary*, as its process is extended into the physical world, diverging concretization through the indeterminacy of material objects. Designed literary objects thus do not merely invite completion through interpretation; they present themselves as materially autonomous presences, evolving their literary enterprise into a fictional hylomorphic hypothesis.

Even if these objects, without a doubt, withhold and provide a basis for a diverse set of indeterminacies in the face of individuals, when an object exists both within a text and externally as a designed artifact, its phenomenological encounter is no longer limited to reading—it extends into the tactile, visual, and spatial. Thus, the emancipated physical object is capable of generating, or functioning within, its own truth conditions, moving beyond its fictional qualities or its *perceivable* or *interpretable* fictional qualities. For instance, a wooden "object-sonnet" can cast shadows, age, acquire patinas, and occupy specific spatial coordinates on a shelf between books authored by Calvino, Borges, Spinoza, or other real authors.

This raises questions like: can such objects still be considered "fictional"? If so, how do these amphibious fictional objects—existing between text and object—manifest in experience? Such entities are neither purely abstract nor merely material. Even when their fictionality persists, it coexists with a form of actualization. Drawing from Meinong's distinction between existence and subsistence, one might argue that prior to fabrication, these objects subsist as intentional objects—quasi or abstract entities posited by a text. Once fabricated, however, they take on multiple statuses to become fictional hylomorphisms (imaginary impositions of mind shaping matter) that are altogether concrete and actual (physical artifacts), abstract and fictional (manifestations of a narrative function).

From this perspective, we are no longer dealing with "objects" in a traditional sense. Instead, we confront amphibious fictional entities, things that straddle multiple modes of being without fully belonging to any single one. Thus, could these objects shed the category of "object" altogether?! Could they evolve into something other than mere material arrangements of atoms, constituting a form predicated in fiction rather than in objecthood? Terms that arise in the attempt to classify them include: fictional noumenon, fictional hylomorphism, paraobjects, fictionalized objects, inter-objects, pseudo-objects, objects from a fictional non-fiction, unreal-real objects, maybe-objects, boundary objects, pataphysical objects, metafictional objects, parafictional objects, amphibious objects (this list must be acknowledged as heuristic rather than classificatory. Its extension arises from the failure of existing ontological categories to accommodate these hybrid beings.)

Even if one departs from the premise that the objects in this *Commentary* are indeed some-kind-of-object, one could push further and claim that no matter how closely an actual object resembles its fictional counterpart, the actual object would never be the fictional object itself, but rather an obscured shadow, an imperfect copy of its ideal form. Thus, there might not be such a thing as an object-sonnet, but rather a (1) written object-sonnet, a (2) printed object-sonnet, a (3) wooden object-sonnet, a (4) reader's imagined object-sonnet, and (5) other—yet to be realized—instantiations of whatever an object-sonnet could be. A fictional *Designed Literature* thus resists and contradicts itself through an unavoidable multiplicity, allowing for a *phenomenonto-logical* pluralism wherein objects are simultaneously written, visual, fictional, historical, actual, non-actual, imagined, realized, possible, impossible, real, unreal, material, and conceptual, among others.

This pluralism could be counter-argued by the type/token distinction, exclusively resorting to a phenomenological explanation—where such objects are seen as having multiple instantiations or adumbrations rather than distinct ontological statuses. These might suggest, via the type/token distinction, that the fictional "object-sonnet" functions as a type instantiated in multiple tokens: textual, visual, material. But unlike ordinary types, the fictional type here is constituted retroactively through its instantiations. Here, a paradox emerges: the object-sonnet depends on the real sonnet-type to exist at all, yet repositions the written sonnet not as the type itself, but as just one among several tokens that enact the fiction differently. Thus, unless one of the object-sonnet tokens explicitly addresses its fictionality, the real type risks being dissolved. This invites a distributed ontology, where each manifestation is a partial disclosure of an object whose being is never fully present in any one form—provoking varied modes of engagement, clashing through the rules of the different discourses it engages with, forming a complex experiential structure that neither literature nor design alone could provide.

In this light, Markus Gabriel's assertion in *Fields of Sense: A New Realist Ontology*: "Some things are objects within a field and simultaneously a field in which objects appear, and there is a sense in which fields take priority over objects even though both are necessary for something to appear, to exist" explains how objects appear only within fields of sense; structured domains in which meaning and existence are co-constituted. Thus, it could be stipulated that a designed literary fiction, produces its own hybrid field, wherein the object is shaped neither solely by the logic of literature nor that of design, but by their friction. This results in a new condition of appearance that exceeds the capacities of both (the question then is no longer what the object is nor how it appears, but what emerges between these). Consequently, it becomes challenging to determine whether our descriptions of phenomena truly reflect the world or are merely extensions of particular localized fields, customs, assumptions, and beliefs.   *

In this manner, if both design and literature have different strategies for constituting meaning, and *designed literature* is a relay system that hypothesizes within these fields, the ontological question—what is this object?!—becomes inseparable from the phenomenological or epistemological one—how do we know or experience it?! The boundary between the real and the imaginary is no longer a divide, but a fictional affordance; a lens through which fiction organizes phenomena.

In sum, *designed literature* does not merely fabricate fiction; it expands the very machinery through which fiction emerges. Its hypotheses generate objects of understanding through construction and manipulation, deploying fictional heuristics and speculative epistemologies that resist reductive functionalism. Therefore, is the tension between design and literature confined solely to ontological or phenomenological concerns, or does it also implicate their epistemic relationship within the act of designing literature? Could models of designed literature, functioning as relay systems between design and literary practice, offer new ways of manipulating the boundaries imposed between the real and the imaginary?

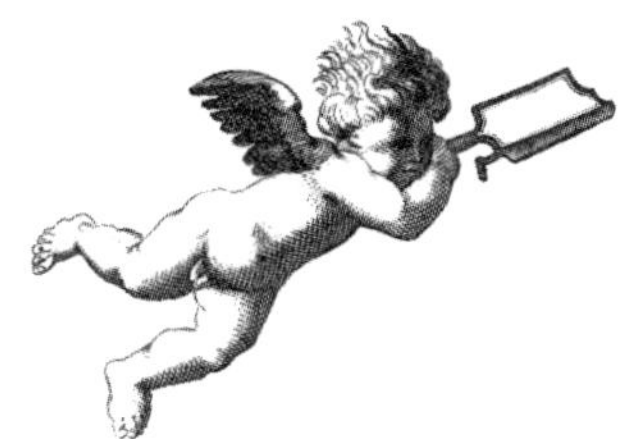

Set Margins number: 57
Title: Commentary on *Approximations to the Object*
Subtitle: An Inquiry into Designed Literature
Author: Pedro Bernstein

ISBN:978-90-835325-0-9
Contributing authors: Edmund Stone
Contributing editors: Courtney Smith
Contributing dramaturgist: Florencio Noceti
Translator: Pedro Bernstein
Graphic design: Pedro Bernstein
Text editor: Pedro Bernstein
1ˢᵗ Proofreader: Courtney Smith
2ⁿᵈ: Proofreader Martina Graña
Image editor: Pedro Bernstein
Editorial Design Assistant: Irene Casado
Printer: Printon, Tallin (Est.)
Fonts: EB Garamond, Krungthep Regular,
Nicholas Cochin LT Pro Black,
Stix General, Stix Two Math

This project was made possible thanks to the generous support of
Freek Loome and Set Margins.

I would also like to thank Florencio Noceti, Courtney Smith, Mia Finkman,
Martina Graña, Irene Casado, Killeen Hanson, Martino Manca,
Susan Yelavich, Anthony Dunne, Clara Prat Gay, William Sumrall, Florencia
Wertheimer, and Pablo Bernstein for their generosity, critical conversations
and encouragement throughout the process.

Set Margins'
www.setmargins.press

Pedro Bernstein
www.pedrobernstein.com